eating Shakespeare

Recipes and More from the Bard's Kitchen

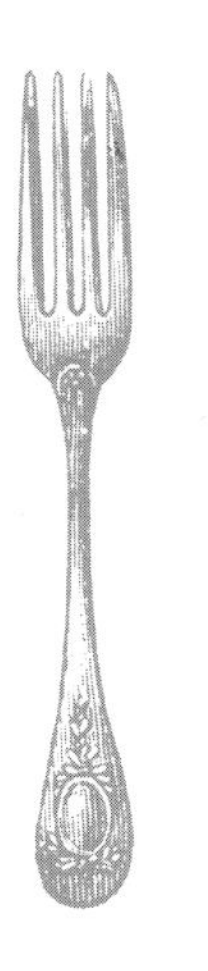

Betty + Sonia Zyvatkauskas

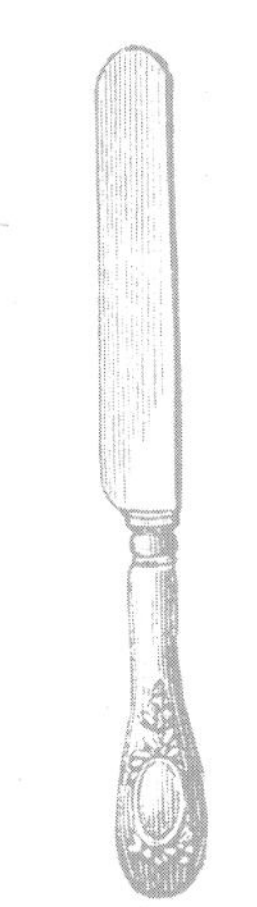

A Pearson Company
Toronto

To Mum, with thanks

Canadian Cataloguing in Publication Data

Zyvatkauskas, Betty
Eating Shakespeare: recipes and more from the bard's kitchen

Includes index.
ISBN 0-13-089452-4

1. Cookery, English – Early works to 1800. I. Zyvatkauskas, Sonia. II. Title.

TX705.Z98 2000 641.5942'09'031 C00-931465-2

ISBN 0-13-089452-4

Editorial Director, Trade Division: Andrea Crozier
Acquisitions Editor: Nicole de Montbrun
Copy Editor: Susan Broadhurst
Production Editor: Jodi Lewchuk
Art Direction: Mary Opper
Cover and Interior Design: Sharon Foster
Production Manager: Kathrine Pummell
Page Layout: Kyle Gell

Woodcut image used by permission of the Henry E. Huntington Library, San Marino, California.

1 2 3 4 5 KR 04 03 02 01 00

Printed and bound in Canada.

Visit the Prentice Hall Canada Web site! Send us your comments, browse our catalogues, and more. www.phcanada.com.

Contents

Chronology

1558 ✦ Elizabeth I ascends the throne.

1564 ✦ **William Shakespeare born.**
✦ Captain John Hawkins brings the sweet potato back from South America.

1569 ✦ The sale of raw fruit is forbidden in London during plague outbreak.

1575 ✦ *A Proper New Booke of Cookery* printed in London.

1588 ✦ Shakespeare marries Anne Hathaway.
✦ Spanish Armada defeated.
✦ Robert May (author of *The Accomplisht Cook*) born.

1591 ✦ *A Booke of Cookrye with the Serving in of the Table* printed in London.

1592 ✦ Shakespeare fully immersed in theatrical world. *1 Henry VI* performed at the Rose Theatre, London.
✦ Plague outbreak in London from summer 1592 to June 1594 causes theatres to close.

1594 ✦ *The Good Huswifes Handmaide for the Kitchin* printed in London.

1595 ✦ The first orange trees in England are planted in Surrey.
✦ During the summer Londoners riot over sudden increases in the price of food due to poor harvests and market speculation.

1596 ✦ Hugh Platt releases *Sundrie New and Artificial Remedies against Famine.*
✦ *The Good Huswifes Jewell* by Thomas Dawson, revised, printed in London.
✦ *The Herball or General Historie of Plantes* by John Gerard published.

1598 ✦ *Epulario, or the Italian Banquet* translated into English and printed in London.

1599 ✦ The Globe Theatre opens as the most lavish playhouse in London, with William Shakespeare owning a one-tenth share.

1600 ✦ East India Company established to trade spices.
✦ *Delightes for Ladies* by Sir Hugh Platt printed in London.

1603 ✦ Queen Elizabeth I dies; succeeded by James I.

1615 ✦ *A New Booke of Cookerie* by John Murrell printed in London.
✦ *The English Housewife* by Gervase Markham printed in London.

1616 ✦ **(April 23) Shakespeare dies.**

1617 ✦ *A Daily Exercise for Ladies and Gentlewomen* by John Murrell printed in London.

1623 ✦ Shakespeare's collected works printed in London.

1625 ✦ James I dies; Charles I ascends to the throne.

1629 ✦ *Paridisi in Sole* by herbalist John Parkinson printed in London.

1642–48 ✦ The Great Rebellion

1649–58 ✦ Commonwealth, Oliver Cromwell Lord Protector.

1660 ✦ Restoration of the Stuart dynasty under Charles II.
✦ *The Accomplisht Cook or The Art and Mystery of Cookery* by Robert May first published.

1672 ✦ *The Accomplisht Ladys Delight* by Hannah Woolley published.

Introduction

SHAKESPEARE'S WORKS abound with colourful references to food, both comic and poetic. Eating is one of life's great commonalties. For both the bawdy crowds who paid a penny to stand in the pit of the Globe Theatre and Queen Elizabeth I herself, the metaphors of food were universally understood. Calling someone a "beef brain" carries the same impact today that it did in 1600.

Scholars have variously suggested that Shakespeare must have been a lawyer, horse groom, or soldier because he writes so authoritatively about these fields. We know that Shakespeare wasn't a cook, but he certainly ate the food of his day, from the London cookhouses and taverns to the noble tables of his friend the Earl of Southampton. This relationship is carried into his plays. In ribald tavern scenes Falstaff and Mistress Quickly touch on day-to-day life: serving illicit meat on fish days, enjoying a bedtime cup of posset, or eating anchovies while drinking ale and sack. In more regal settings Prince Hamlet talks of the pies served at his father's funeral, Anthony and Cleopatra are said to eat gigantic breakfasts, and Prince Troilus is given a lesson in patience in Pandarus's exposition on making cake.

Shakespeare's lower-class characters seem to relish food, while for nobility food becomes a metaphor for the corrupt: Lady Macbeth poisons the posset and Titus Andronicus cooks his enemies in a pie. Henry VI longs to experience the simple pleasure of a humble repast:

> *...the shepherd's homely curds,*
> *His cold thin drink out of his leather bottle,*
> *His wonted sleep under a fresh tree's shade,*
> *All which secure and sweetly he enjoys,*

Is far beyond a prince's delicates,
His viands sparkling in a golden cup,
His body couched in a curious bed,
When care, mistrust, and treason waits on him.

Shakespeare was known for his great staging, and what better moment for a theatrical denouement than a great battle or a great feast, when virtually all of the characters are onstage?

Food provides more than sustenance. It gives pleasure and creates a setting for social bonding. By approaching period recipes through the poetry of Shakespeare we celebrate the Elizabethan relationship to food and tailor it to modern palates. In this cookbook we introduce readers to foods commonly enjoyed by Elizabethans, using authentic period recipes and Shakespearean references.

Elizabethan dishes, though still close to medieval, included more imported foods and new varieties of vegetables and fruits. It was a period of exploration that saw the introduction of potatoes from the Americas and many new varieties of greens, including asparagus and artichokes from Europe.

Many of the spices (cinnamon, nutmeg, mace, and cloves) seem familiar to modern cooks but are used in ways that are unusual to us. Cinnamon flavours a veal stew. Ginger and cinnamon are mixed into cooked salad greens. Nutmeg appears with scallops. Rosewater and other floral preparations appear in highly perfumed dishes.

These recipes reflect the food crazes of the day. The obsession with oranges, a popular theatre snack, was carried over into the kitchen. Their juice was transformed into sauces for roast meats, and slices of oranges were squeezed over crispy fritters. Meats were sprinkled with sugar and cooked with dried fruits such as currants, raisins, and dates for additional sweetness. Currants and raisins were used profusely, even in meat dishes, to satisfy the growing lust for all things sweet. Some items have since fallen out of use, such as the glandular scents of ambergreese and musk, now replaced by vanilla.

In modifying these recipes for modern cooks we have tried to remain true to the spirit of the period while accommodating modern tastes. For example, we have omitted most of the suet and radically reduced the butter. In transcribing the period recipes we have used a modern alphabet but kept most of the colourful Elizabethan spellings.

The Cooks and Their Recipes

Robert May

Born in 1588 during the reign of Queen Elizabeth I, Robert May began his long culinary career as a boy under the tutelage of his father, who was also a professional cook. One of his early patrons sent him to France, where he worked for a prominent Parisian family for five years before returning to England. After a career that spanned half a century, he wrote *The Accomplisht Cook, or the Art and Mystery of Cookery,* a comprehensive culinary guide intended for fellow professionals.

Educated, multilingual, and well travelled, May was familiar with French, Italian, and Spanish techniques, although he remained fiercely nationalistic, referring to "other Nations, who in the Art fall short of what I have known experimented by you my worthy Countreymen."

The Accomplisht Cook provides hundreds of recipes ranging from a Spanish stew called Olio Podrida, to bread puddings, boiled larks, pickled cucumbers, and elaborate pies filled with live animals as a practical joke to delight dinner guests. May was employed by prosperous London gentry and minor nobles at a time when the growing commercial class experienced unprecedented prosperity and engaged in lavish entertaining. As May noted, "To be confined and limited to the narrowness of a Purse is to want the Materials from which the Artist must gain his knowledge."

May lived through the reigns of four monarchs, a civil war, and the intervening rule of parliament and the Puritans under Oliver Cromwell. He reminisced fondly about what he saw as the golden age of English hospitality in the early 1600s.

He dismisses previous cookbooks as "to very little purpose, empty and unprofitable Treatises" due to the "confusion of the Method, or the barrenness of those Authour's Experience."

Hugh Platt

Sir Hugh Platt might well be one such author lacking in actual kitchen experience. Although he wrote three books that include recipes his grasp of cooking techniques is not his forte. The recipes are usually more inventive than practical and Platt can best be described as an entrepreneur or "idea man."

Along with his recipes for syrup of roses and candied marigolds, Platt instructs readers how to "make many little fishes out of one great and nautrall fish" by mixing their flesh with gelatin and crumbs. He offers the Royal Navy a bizarre suggestion for preserving beef on long voyages: towing barrels of it behind the ships.

With all the salesmanship of a Shopping Channel huckster he promises readers even more...if only they buy his next book, treatise, or instructions for many of his incredible devices such as a portable sauna connected to one's chimney.

Knighted late in his career, Platt was probably quite well travelled, as is suggested by his knowledge of pasta and mustard. He was a self-made man. Born in 1552 to a London brewer, he died a wealthy landowner, typifying the rise of the new middle class. He was most respected for his horticultural research.

Gervase Markham

A complete contrast to Platt, Gervase Markham is a down-to-earth writer full of practical advice on matters of animal husbandry and "huswifely" duties. Addressing readers who may think a man to be "out of his element" writing about women's work, Markham claims to be editing the recipes given to him by a woman "singular among those of her rank." *The English Huswife,* part of a larger work called *Countrey Countentments* published in 1615, covers a range of housekeeping matters with a special emphasis on cookery.

Markham's sensible advice on transplanting herbs, making hippocras, and frying pancakes was widely read and reprinted many times throughout his life. In fact, there was no remainder bin for Markham's books. He was notorious for taking old, unsold volumes and reissuing them under new titles. He did this so often that booksellers made him sign a letter promising not to write any more books on the subject of cattle and horses.

Shakespeare probably used Markham's horse expertise in the course of researching his plays. The list of horse diseases in *The Taming of the Shrew* is generally attributed to one of Markham's tracts on animal husbandry.

Markham also dabbled in the theatre and co-authored several minor works. He and Shakespeare travelled in the same circles, both of them friends to the Earl of Southampton and the Earl of Essex.

John Murrell

In *A New Booke of Cookerie,* published in 1615, John Murrell devotes a special chapter to London Cookerie, with slightly more sophisticated offerings representing the culinary range of the quickly growing urban centre.

A professional cook, Murrell honed his craft during his travels in France, Italy, and the "Low Countries." He also wrote *A Daily Exercise for Ladies and Gentlewomen.*

Giovanne de Rosselli

Just as Elizabethan fashion and architecture borrowed ideas from the continent, so too did cuisine. Hence the popularity of the 1598 translation of *Epulario, or the Italian Banquet* by "A.J." from the 1516 original by Giovanne de Rosselli. In addition to providing instructions on the making of pasta and a variation of polenta, *Epulario* contains such continental recipes as "To make mustard after the manner of Padoa" and "To make a new dish after the manner of Rome."

John Partridge

In addition to several histories rendered in verse, Partridge wrote *The Treasurie of Hidden Secrets.* He is also attributed as the author of *Good Huswifes Handmaide for the Kitchin.*

Thomas Dawson

Dawson is the author of *The Good Huswifes Jewell,* published in 1596. Little is known about him. One source suggests that he was not a writer but a printer of books. *The Good Huswifes Jewell* contains innovative recipes such as lemon salad and one of the earliest potato recipes, "A Tart to Provoke Courage."

Hannah Woolley

Although Elizabethan cookbooks often attribute individual recipes to women, Hannah Woolley is the only acknowledged female author of an entire cookbook in this period. Woolley was employed as a servant and teacher. In addition to *The Accomplisht Ladys Delight,* printed in 1672, she wrote four other books on similar subjects.

Soups, Stews, and Pottages

Cherry Soup

When he beheld his shadow in the brook,
The fishes spread it on their golden gills;
When he was by, the birds such pleasure took,
That some would sing, some, in their bills
Would bring him mulberries and ripe-red cherries:
He fed them with his sight, they him with berries.
—Venus and Adonis

Sops of buttery toast serve as a counterpoint to the sour cherries in this dessert soup.

To make pottage of Cherries

from *A Book of Cookrye* by A.W.

Fry white bread in butter til it be brown and so put it into a dish, then take Cherries and take out the stones, and frye them where you fried the bread, then put thereto Sugar, Ginger, and Sinamon, for lack of broth, take White or Claret Wine, boyle these togither, and that doon, serve them upon your Tostes.

CHERRY CHICANERY

Cherries, a much-loved fruit, were made into tarts, pastes (fruit leathers), and syrups as well as being dried, preserved, and candied. Their popularity may be attested to by the fact that 600 cherry trees were once planted in the orchard at Hampton Court, the royal palace.

Receiving a royal visit was considered to be the highest honour, and hosts fell over themselves looking for new ways to earn the queen's admiration. In one instance, Sir Francis Carew covered a cherry tree in his orchard with a canvas tarp to delay the fruit's ripening. Shortly before her majesty's arrival, he exposed the cherries to the sun, so while all of the other cherry trees in England had long since dropped their fruit, he led Queen Elizabeth I to his fruitful surprise, much to her delight.

Our Version

6 slices good-quality white bread (such as French stick), crusts removed
Butter, for frying
28-ounce jar pitted cherries in their juice
¼ cup sugar
2 teaspoons ground ginger
3 teaspoons cinnamon
½ cup white wine (optional)

Sauté slices of bread in butter until golden-brown. Place each slice in the bottom of a soup bowl. Simmer cherries and juice in a stainless steel or enamel pan. Add the sugar, ginger, cinnamon, and wine (if using) to the cherries and simmer for 15 minutes. Ladle the soup into bowls over the fried bread.

KNAVISH NURSERYMEN

John Parkinson, who wrote extensively on gardening, had a very low opinion of nursery employees. He complained that they often took saplings of Flanders Cherries and sold them as the highly prized May Cherries. Apparently they were even more unscrupulous when it came to rarer species, as Parkinson notes, "scarce one in twenty of our Nurserie men doe sell the right, but give one for another: for it is an inherent qualitie almost hereditarie with most of them, to sell any man an ordinary fruit for whatsoever rare fruit he shall aske for: so little they are to be trusted."

Onion Soup

...eat no onions nor garlic, for we are to utter sweet breath; and I do not doubt but to hear them say it is a sweet comedy.

—A Midsummer Night's Dream

ONION EYES

My tongue shall utter all, mine
eyes like sluices,
As from a mountain spring that
feeds a dale,
Shall gush pure streams to purge
my impure tale.

—*The Rape of Lucrece*

Thynges which do hurt the eyes:

Drunkennesse

Lecherye

Muste

All pulse

Sweet wynes, and thycke wynes

Hempe sede

Very salte meates

Garlyke

Onyons

Colewortes

Radyshe

Reedynge after supper immediately

—Thomas Elyot, *The Castel of Health,* 1541

A Sop of Onions

from *The Good Huswifes Jewell* by Thomas Dawson

Take and slice your Onions, put them in a frying panne with a dish or two of sweete butter, and frie them together, then take a litle faire water and put into it salt and peper, and so frie them together a little more, then boile them in a lyttle Earthen pot, putting to it a lyttle water and sweet butter, etc. You may use Spinnage in like manner.

Our Version

4 onions, sliced, about 6 cups (try mixing different varieties, such as French shallots, sweet Vidalia, and yellow cooking onions)	¼ pound butter 3 cups water or chicken stock 1 teaspoon salt ¼ teaspoon pepper

Sauté onions in butter until they turn a rich golden-brown and begin to form a gluey mass (about 15 to 20 minutes). Stir often. Add water or stock, salt, and pepper. Bring to a boil and simmer for 20 to 30 minutes. Adjust seasonings.

Serving suggestion: Serve with large croutons of toasted whole wheat bread.

ONION DECONGESTANT

Inhaling onion juice up the nose was said to "purge the head very-well." If you preferred, you could always mix the juice with a little vinegar and use it as a skin cleanser, a cure for insomnia, or a laxative.

round Beef with Nuts

Bread was the chief starch served at the Elizabethan table, usually presented as a sop to soak up broth (hence the word soup) or a sippet, a more daintily carved piece of toast or fried bread.

This simple recipe, served on sippets, is a sort of Elizabethan Sloppy Joe.

BEEF BRAIN

Thersites: The plague of Greece upon thee, thou mongrel beef-witted lord!

—Troilus and Cressida

Looking for an epicurean epithet to hurl at your enemy? Try these gastronomic put-downs from the master of insults himself:

Greasy knight

Bread chipper

Salt-butter rogue

Knave, rascal, eater of broken meats

Unwholesome humidity, gross wat'ry pumpion

Crusty batch of nature

Trencher-knight

Hash of raw Beef

from *The Accomplisht Cook* by Robert May

Mince it very small with some beef-suet or lard, some sweet herbs, pepper, salt, some cloves and mace, blanched chesnuts, or almonds blanched, and put in whole, some nutmeg, and a whole onion or two, and stew it finely in a pipkin with some strong broth the space of two hours; put a little claret to it, and serve it on sippets finely carved, with some grapes or lemon in it also, or barberries, and blow off the fat.

Our Version

1 tablespoon lard or oil
1 pound lean ground beef
¼ teaspoon ground nutmeg
½ teaspoon ground mace
¼ teaspoon ground cloves
1-½ cups beef stock
½ cup red wine
¼ cup chestnuts or almonds
1 whole onion
Sprigs of parsley
Sprigs of thyme
3 bay leaves
Salt and pepper, to taste
Toast
Grapes or lemon slices, for garnish

Melt the lard or oil in a saucepan and brown the ground beef. Add the spices. Add the stock, wine, chestnuts or almonds, and the onion. Tie the parsley, thyme, and bay leaves into a bouquet with kitchen twine and add to the meat. Add the salt and pepper. Simmer for about 45 minutes. Remove the onion and bouquet and adjust the seasoning. Skim off any fat and serve on toast, garnished with grapes or lemon slices.

WHET YOUR WIT

Lest someone call you a beef brain, here's a mind-sharpening elixir from *The English Housewife:* "To quicken a mans wits, spirits and memory; let him take Langdebeefe, which is gathered in June or July, and beating it in a cleane morter; let him drinke the juyce thereof with warme water, and hee shall finde the benefit."

Stewed Lamb with Carrots

England was a major wool-producing country so mutton, the meat of mature sheep, was abundant. Modern cooks may use lamb in this simple stew that derives its rich flavour from lavish quantities of fresh herbs. Along with the savory and thyme, Elizabethan cooks would have included hyssop, a pretty and aromatic plant whose bitter leaves can be eaten in a salad or added to gamey meats. Hyssop is reputed to aid digestion.

To boyle Mutton with Carrets

from *The Good Huswifes Handmaide for the Kitchin* attributed to John Partridge

Take a breast or necke of Mutton, cut it of the bignes of your thombe, and put it into an earthern pot with faire water, and make it seeth: Then take Carret rootes, and scrape them cleane, and cut them of the bignes of your Mutton. and let them seeth, then put in half a handfull of stripped Tyme, as much of Savorie and Isope, and a litle salte and Pepper: Let them seeth till your Mutton and roots be verie tender, then serve them upon sops.

OF VERBS AND ROOTS

This comic Latin grammar lesson quickly degenerates into double meaning when Mistress Quickly joins in:

William: Articles are borrow'd of the pronoun, and be thus declin'd: *'Singulariter, nominativo, hic, haec, hoc.'*

Evans: *'Nominativo, hig, hag, hog.'* Pray you mark: *'genitivo, hujus.'* Well, what is your accusative case?

William: *'Accusativo, hinc.'*

Evans: I Pray you have your remembrance child. Accusative, *hung, hang, hog.*

Quickly: 'Hang-hog' is Latin for bacon, I warrant you.

Evans: Leave your prabbles, 'oman. What is the focative case, William?

William: *'O, vocativo, O.'*

Evans: Remember, William; focative is *'caret.'*

Quickly: And that's a good root.

—*The Merry Wives of Windsor*

Our Version

4 lamb shoulder chops (about 12 oz after trimming)	1 or 2 tablespoons olive oil
1 teaspoon salt	2–3 cups water
½ teaspoon pepper	Sprigs of fresh thyme
2–3 tablespoons flour	Sprigs of fresh savory
	3 or 4 carrots, peeled and sliced

Trim the meat, carefully removing fat and tough membranes, then cut it into ½-inch cubes. Mix the salt and pepper in the flour and dredge the pieces of lamb. Pour the olive oil in a saucepan and brown the lamb over medium to high heat, being careful to brown the flour without burning it. Pour in the water and stir well. Tie the springs of thyme and savory together to make a bouquet, and put that in the pot with the lamb. Cook for about 45 minutes over slow heat. Top up with water, as necessary. Add the carrots to the stew and continue to cook for another 30 minutes. The stew is ready when both the carrots and the meat are tender.

Serving suggestion: Serve with thick slices of fresh whole wheat bread.

A CARROT FOR YOUR CAP

Herbalist John Parkinson offers this interesting observation on the fashion uses of the orange root: "The Carrot hath many winged leaves, rising from the head of the roote, which are much cut and divided into many other leaves, and they also cut and divided into many parts, of a deepe greene colour, some whereof in Autumne will turne to be of a fine red or purple (the beautie whereof allureth many Gentlewomen oftentimes to gather the leaves, and sticke them in their hats or heads, or pin them on their armes in stead of feathers)."

Green Pea Soup with Bacon

This fellow pecks up wit as pigeons peas,
And utters it again when God doth please.
—Love's Labour's Lost

This bright green soup would have been especially appealing to Elizabethan diners who adored brilliant colours.

Pottage in the Italian Fashion

from *The Accomplisht Cook* by Robert May

Boil green pease with some strong broth, and interlarded bacon cut into slices; the pease being boild, put to them some chopped parsley, pepper, anniseed, and strain some of the pease to thicken the broth: give it a walm and serve it on sippets; with boild chickens, pigeons, kids, or lambs head, mutton, duck, mallard, or any poultrey.

Sometimes for variety you may thicken the broth with eggs.

NON-SMOKING BACON, PLEASE

For the Elizabethan cook who lacked the benefits of modern ventilation, Hugh Platt has this typically colourful and impractical advice on preventing smoke when broiling bacon or other meats: "Make little dripping pannes of paper: pasting up the corners with starch or paste, wet them a little in water, but Pope Pius Quintas his Cooke will have them touched over with a feather first dipped in oyle or molten butter, lay them on your gridiron, and place therin your slices of bacon, turning them as you see cause. This is a cleanly way, and avoideth all smoke...You must be careful that your fire under the gridiron flame not, least you happen to burne your dripping pannes..."

Hotspur: O, he is as tedious
As a tired horse, a railing wife,
Worse than a smoky house.

—*1 Henry IV*

Our Version

3 rashers bacon, finely diced
2-½ cups frozen green peas
2-½ cups hot chicken stock
2 tablespoons chopped parsley
¼ teaspoon aniseed
Pinch of pepper

Fry the diced bacon until crispy and drain off the fat. Place peas, stock, and bacon in a soup pot and simmer for 15 minutes. Take 1-½ cups (approximately half of the soup) and purée it in a blender, then return it to the pot. Add parsley, aniseed, and pepper. Adjust seasonings and simmer for another 5 minutes.

Lamb Stewed with Ale

Would I were in an alehouse in London,
I would give all my fame for a pot of ale and safety.
—Henry V

The dried fruits in this recipe could be cooked in the pot with the meat, but this dish is more interesting if they are stewed separately to make a chutney-like sauce served on the side.

To make stewed Steakes

from *The Good Huswifes Jewell* by Thomas Dawson

Take a peece of Mutton, and cutte it in peeces, and washe it very cleane, and put it into a faire potte with Ale, or with halfe Wine, then make it boyle, and skumme it cleyne, and put into your pot a faggot of Rosemary and Time, then take some Parsely picked fine, and some onyons cut round, and let them all boyle together, then take prunes, & raisons, dates, and currans, and let it boyle altogether, and season it with Sinamon and Ginger, Nutmeggs, two or three Cloves, and Salt, and so serve it on soppes and garnish it with fruite.

ALEHOUSE WELCOME

Speed: Come on, you madcap, I'll to the alehouse with you presently; where, for one shot of five pence, thou shalt have five thousand welcomes.

—*Two Gentlemen of Verona*

MALTBUGS

William Harrison paints this unflattering portrait of alehouse patrons: "It is incredible to saie how our maltbugs lug at this liquor, even as pigs should lie in a row, lugging at their dames teats, till they lie still againe, and not be able to wag. Neither did Romulus and Remus sucke their shee woolfe, with such eager and sharpe devotion, as these men hale at hufcap, till they be red as cocks, & litle wiser than their combs."

Our Version

1-¾ pounds lamb shoulder	Sprigs of rosemary
Flour, for dredging	Sprigs of thyme
2 tablespoons olive oil	Sprigs of parsley
2 cups ale	1 onion, sliced into thin rounds
½ teaspoon salt	

FRUIT SAUCE

6 prunes, pitted and cut in quarters	¼ teaspoon grated nutmeg
¼ cup raisins	¼ teaspoon ground cloves
6 dates, pitted and sliced	¼ teaspoon ground cinnamon
1 tablespoon currants	¼ teaspoon ground ginger
	½ cup white wine or water

Trim the fat and membranes from the meat and cut it into ½-inch cubes. Dredge the meat in a little flour. In a 2- or 3-quart saucepan brown the meat in hot oil, then add the ale and salt. Using kitchen twine, tie the herbs into a bouquet and add them to the lamb. Bring to a boil, then simmer for 20 minutes. Add the onion to the lamb and simmer for another 30 minutes.

In the meantime, put the dried fruits and spices in a small saucepan with the wine or water. Bring to a boil while stirring. In a few minutes the mixture will become thick and sticky. Cover the pan and remove from the heat.

Serving suggestion: Serve the meat over slices of bread with a spoonful of fruit sauce on the side. Excellent with Parsnip and Watercress Salad *(see page 22)*.

A PINT OF MAD DOG, PLEASE

According to the traditional division of household labour, brewing and distilling were considered women's work. As a result alehouses had their origins in home businesses set up by women, usually widows in need of an income, who sold ale outside their doors.

The introduction of beer, which required more elaborate brewing equipment, and a rising demand brought on by increased inland traffic forced the alehouse to evolve into a larger, separate establishment.

By the time the alehouse was a regular fixture in London, Elizabethans could order their brews by a number of colourful names, such as Huffecap, Mad Dog, Father Whoresonne, Angels Food, Dragons Milke, Go by the Wall, Stride Wide, and Lift Leg.

Water Gruel

From the witches in Macbeth, *Shakespeare's most famous recipe:*

Round about the cauldron go;
In the poison'd entrails throw;
Toad, that under cold stone
Days and nights has thirty-one
Swelt'red venom, sleeping got,
Boil thou first i' th' charmed pot.
Double, double, toil and trouble;
Fire burn and cauldron bubble.
Fillet of a fenny snake,
In the cauldron boil and bake;
Eye of newt, and toe of frog,
Wool of bat, and tongue of dog,
Adder's fork, and blind-worm's sting,
Lizard's leg, and howlet's wing,
For a charm of pow'rful trouble,
Like a hell-broth boil and bubble.
Double, double, toil and trouble,
Fire burn and cauldron bubble.
Scale of dragon, tooth of wolf,
Witch's mummy, maw and gulf
Of the ravin'd salt-sea shark,
Root of hemlock digg'd i' th' dark,
Liver of blaspheming Jew,
Gall of goat, and slips of yew
Slivered in the moon's eclipse,
Nose of Turk and Tartar's lips,
Finger of birth-strangled babe
Ditch-deliver'd by a drab,

Make the gruel thick and slab.
Add thereto a tiger's chawdron
For th' ingredience of our cau'dron.

Water gruel would have been eaten on fast days. The term gruel *refers to a mixture of ingredients—usually including oatmeal—that was boiled in water. Unlike the witches in* Macbeth, *who boil their gruel "thick and slab," the original recipe is thin and watery. Like the witches, we prefer a more substantial version for breakfast.*

To make Water Gruel

from *The Accomplisht Ladys Delight* by Hannah Woolley

Take a Pottle of Water, a handful of great Oatmeal Pickt, and beat in a Mortar, put it in boyling, when it is half enough, put to it 2 handfuls of Currans washed, a Faggot or 2 of sweet Herbs; 4 or 5 blades of large Mace, and a little sliced Nutmeg, let a grain of Musk be infused a while in it, when it is enough season it with Sugar and Rose-water, and put to it a little drawn butter.

Our Version

2 pints water
1 cup oatmeal
½ cup raisins
¼ cup currants
1 teaspoon nutmeg
Sugar, to taste
2 drops rosewater (optional)

Combine all of the ingredients in a saucepan. Bring to a boil, then simmer until the desired consistency is achieved, stirring frequently.

LET THEM HAUL WATER

In Shakespeare's time, there was no running water in households. Throughout London, water was held in large cisterns fed by a series of conduits. From there, the water had to be carried home. Those who could afford it hired water-haulers. "Cobs," or "cocks" as they were known, were a common sight along the narrow streets, carrying large wooden buckets on their shoulders. With little status and even lower pay, they had a reputation for being unruly. In one instance, several men were whipped for cutting the lead pipes and shutting off the water in most of London.

The *Chronicles of England* contains a typical example of the provisions commonly made for the poor in Elizabethan wills. Holinshed makes his opinion about the poor quite clear, although in this case it would be hard to blame the recipients if they were less than grateful. He writes that William Lambe, "seeing the hardnesse of this age wherein we live, that manie would worke if they have meanse...hath bene thus beneficiall to poore women that are glad to take pains, as to bestow a hundred and twentie pales, wherewith to carrie and serve water: an honest shift of living, though somewhat toilesome."

Hodgepodge

Mrs. Page: Why, Sir John, do you think, though we would have thrust virtue out of our hearts by the head and shoulders, and have given ourselves without scruple to hell, that ever the devil could have made you our delight?
Ford: What, a hodge-pudding? A bag of flax?
Mrs. Page: A puff'd man?
—The Merry Wives of Windsor

The origins of the popular pub grub the Lancashire hotpot can be seen in these economical stews that were made by adding whatever roots were on hand to stew with a bit of mutton.

To make a Hodgepodge

from *A Book of Cookrye* by A.W.

Boyle a neck of Mutton or a fat rump of Beef, and when it is well boyled, take the best of the broth and put it into a pipkin and put a good many onyons to it, two handfull of marigold flowers, and a handful of percely fine picked and groce shredde and not too small, and so boyle them in the broth and thicke it with strained bread, putting therin groce beaten pepper, and a spoonfull of Vinagre, and let it boyle somewhat thick and so lay it upon your meat.

PLEASE BE SEATED

Diners were seated at the table according to a strict hierarchy. Only the most honoured guest had his own chair; everyone else shared benches or sat on stools.

If there were no diners equal to your rank, you sat at your own table. At his coronation dinner Macbeth instructs his guests to find their places according to status: "You know your own degrees, sit down." They would have arranged themselves according to the following guidelines:

Group 1: archbishops, cardinals, emperors, kings, princes, and dukes

Group 2: bishops, marquises, and earls

Group 3: viscounts, legates, barons, chief justices, and the Lord Mayor of London

Group 4: cathedral priors, archdeacons, knights, deans, clerks of the crown, and the Mayor of Callais

Group 5: preachers, parsons, vicars, city bailiffs, a sergeant at arms, merchants, gentlemen, and an ex-mayor of London.

To make a Hotch-Pot

from *The Accomplisht Ladys Delight* by Hannah Woolley

Take a piece of Brisket of Beef, a piece of Mutton, a Knuckle of Veal, a good Cullender of Pot-herbs, half minced Carrots, Onions and Cabbage, a little broken, boyl all these together untill they be very thick.

Our Version

1–1-½ pounds stewing beef (such as blade steak)
1 pound lamb shoulder (about 3 large chops)
Flour, for dredging
3 tablespoons oil
4 cups beef stock
1 teaspoon dried thyme
½ teaspoon dried savory
½ teaspoon pepper
1 tablespoon red wine vinegar
4 carrots, peeled and sliced
3 onions, peeled and diced
¼ cabbage, roughly chopped
½ cup chopped parsley

Cut the meat into 1-inch cubes. Dredge it in a little flour, then sauté it in oil until browned. Add the stock, thyme, savory, pepper, and vinegar. Cook for 30 minutes, then add the carrots, onions, and cabbage. Cook for another 30 minutes. Stir occasionally; if it looks too dry, add more beef stock or water. Add the chopped parsley just before serving.

Diverse Salads

A Grand Salad

This carefully arranged salad can be made with any combination of the ingredients listed. The original calls for samphire, an aromatic herb whose succulent leaves were traditionally pickled, and broom buds, a medicinal herb used to make yellow fabric dye. We've replaced these with chopped parsley, but other fresh herbs or pickles may be used instead of, or in addition to, the parsley.

To make a grand Sallet of divers Compounds

from *The Accomplisht Cook* by Robert May

Take a cold roast capon and cut it into thin slices square and small, (or any other rost meat, as chicken, mutton, veal, or neats tongue) mingle with it a little minced taragon and an onion; then mince lettice as small as the capon, mingle all together, and lay it in the middle of a clean scowred dish. Then lay capers by themselves, olives by themselves, samphire by it self, broom-buds, pickled mushrooms, pickled oysters, lemon, orange, raisins, almonds, blew figs, Virginia Potato, caperons, crucifex pease, and the like, more or les, as occasion serves, lay them by themselves in the dish round the meat in partitions. Then garnish the dish sides with quarters of oranges and lemons, or in slices, oyls and vinegar beaten together, and poured on it over all.

On fish dayes, a roast broild or boild pike, boned, and being cold, slice it as abovesaid.

LETTUCE AND THE LIBIDO

In Shakespeare's day "sallet" referred to any edible leafy green.

Cade: ...These five days have I hid me in these woods and durst not peep out, for all the country is laid for me; but now I am so hungry that, if I might have a lease of my life for a thousand years, I could stay no longer. Wherefore, on a brick wall have I climb'd into this garden, to see if I can eat grass, or pick a sallet another while, which is not amiss to cool a man's stomach this hot weather.

—2 Henry VI

The cooling effect of lettuce was also noted by Dr. Andrew Boorde in his *Dyettary of Helth,* dated 1542. Despite his claims that lettuce also caused drowsiness and decreased the libido, the Elizabethans were not deterred from enjoying a rich variety of garden greens.

Our Version

For the Centre of the Platter

- 1 cold cooked chicken, or 4 cold cooked chicken breasts, diced
- 1 green onion, chopped
- 2 teaspoons fresh tarragon leaves, chopped
- 1 head leaf lettuce, shredded

Radiating from the Centre

- ¼ cup capers
- 1 cup olives
- 2 large potatoes, boiled, then peeled and diced
- 1 cup green peas, blanched
- 2 lemons, peeled and sliced
- 2 oranges, peeled and sliced
- 1 cup parsley, coarsely chopped
- ½ cup sliced almonds, lightly toasted
- ½ cup pickled mushrooms
- 3 ripe figs, quartered
- Additional lemons and oranges, for garnish

Dressing

- ¼ cup good-quality wine vinegar
- ½ cup good-quality olive oil

Mix the chicken with the chopped onion and tarragon and the shredded lettuce. Place the chicken mixture in a mound in the centre of a large platter. Arrange each of the other ingredients in separate rows, radiating outward from the centre of the plate to within 1 inch of the platter. Cut the remaining lemons and oranges into wedges and arrange them around the edge of the platter. Just before serving, mix the vinegar and oil and sprinkle the dressing over the salad.

LETTUCE VARIATIONS

By 1629 herbalist John Parkinson wrote that he knew of 11 or 12 different kinds of lettuce, so many that he doubted people would believe some of them, including Romane red Lettice, Venice Lettice, and Lambes Lettice. He also provided instructions for the home gardener to whiten lettuce and make it more tender to eat, either by piling earth into mounds around the growing plants or by securing the leaves at the top of each bunch with thread.

CODPIECE LINER

One medical treatment calls for lettuce to be applied or bound to the "cods" to "helpeth those that are troubled with the Colts evill," probably a venereal disease. It also tells us that "if a little camphire be added it restraineth immoderate lust."

Parsnip and Watercress Salad

Sweet cooked parsnips on a bed of assorted lettuce makes for an attractive salad with a traditional oil and vinegar dressing. Alexander buds resembled celery and were likely eaten in the same fashion.

ROCKET RUB

According to John Parkinson, warriors, brawlers, or the merely clumsy could treat their bruises with a mixture of crushed rocket seed, a little vinegar, and some ox gall.

Sallet Otherwayes

from *The Accomplisht Cook* by Robert May

Boild parsnips in quarters laid round in the dish, and in the midst some small sallet, or water-cresses finely washed and picked, on the water-cresses some little small lettice finely picked and washed also, then some ellicksander-buds in halves, and some in quarters, and between the quarters of the parsnips some small lettice, some water-cresses, and ellicksander-buds, oyl and vinegar, and round the dish some slices of parsnips.

Our Version

- 3 parsnips, peeled and cut lengthwise into quarters
- 1 small head leaf lettuce
- 1 bunch watercress or arugula
- 2 stalks celery, trimmed and thinly sliced (optional)
- 4 tablespoons olive oil
- 1 tablespoon wine vinegar
- Salt, to taste

Put parsnips in a saucepan with cold water and cook until tender, then drain. Wash and dry the lettuce and watercress. Cut them into bite-sized pieces and arrange them on a large serving plate. Arrange the parsnips and celery, if using, on top of the lettuce and watercress, radiating outward like the spokes of a wheel.

Whisk together the oil, vinegar, and salt, then pour over the salad just before serving.

THE ROOTS THAT WON THE WAR

In *Titus Andronicus,* Aaron, an experienced soldier, plans to raise his infant son in the ways of the warrior.

I'll make you feed on berries
and on roots,
And feed on curds and whey,
and suck the goat,
And cabin in a cave, and bring
you up
To be a warrior and command
a camp.

Fighters foraging for roots in the English countryside might dig up such edibles as turnips, skirrets, or the parsnips that grew near watery bogs.

SAVOURY SALADS

Salads were an essential part of Elizabethan meals, and were thought to provoke an appetite for meat.

Hamlet: ...I remember one said there were no sallets in the lines to make the matter savoury

—*Hamlet*

ooked Salad Greens

Elizabethan salad recipes describe a surprising array of fruits and vegetables. One recipe calls for a salad of mallows, another for burdock roots, and another even for parboiled hop buds.

An excellent all-purpose treatment for a diverse collection of green vegetables is found in John Murrell's A New Booke of Cookerie. *While the original recipe calls for such Elizabethan favourites as rockets, alexanders, and marigold leaves, we found that spinach and watercress make a tasty combination. Asparagus, which had been recently introduced to England, also works well.*

The original version calls for the cooked greens to be served on "sippets," or little pieces of toast, but modern cooks may prefer to serve this as a side dish, as it makes a bold partner to a pork roast.

Divers Sallet Boyled

from *A New Booke of Cookerie* by John Murrell

Parboyl Spinage, and chop it fine, with the edges of two hard trenchers upon a boord, or the backe of two chopping knives: then set them on a Chafing dish of coales with butter and Vinegar. Season it with Sinamon, Ginger, Sugar, and a few parboyled currins. Then cut hard Egges into quarters to garnish it withall, and serve it upon sippets. So may you serve Burrage, Buglosse, Endive, Suckory, Colefowers, Sorrel, Marigold leaves, Water-Cresses, Leeks boyled, Onions, Sparragus, Rocket, Alexanders. Parboyle them, and season them all alike: whether it be with Oyle and Vinegar, or Butter and Vinegar, Sinamon, Ginger, Sugar, and Butter: Egges are necessary, or at least very good for all boyld Sallets.

Our Version

- 1 bag spinach (approximately 10 ounces)
- 1 bunch watercress (adjust to taste, as it lends a peppery flavour)
- ⅛ cup butter
- 1 tablespoon cider vinegar
- ¼ teaspoon cinnamon
- ¼ teaspoon ginger
- 1 tablespoon sugar
- ¼ cup currants, soaked in boiling water, then drained
- 2 hard-boiled eggs, cut into quarters

Parboil spinach and watercress, then drain and chop. Sauté chopped spinach and watercress in butter and vinegar, then season with spices, sugar, and currants. Serve garnished with the hard-boiled eggs.

SPLENDORS OF SPINACH

Spinach appears in a broader range of Elizabethan dishes than any other vegetable, in part due to its lush green colour. Spinach was not only used in salads, but also to fill tarts, colour puddings, stew in pottages, and fry in fritters.

BEASTLY GARNISHES

Animal parts were commonly used to garnish the dishes in which their flesh was served. Swans' heads and necks were left dangling down the sides of raised pies. Peacocks' heads and tail feathers were added to baked peacock pie before serving.

hicken Salad with Apples

Although the garnish of chicken bones is peculiar to the period, the salad itself has stood the test of time.

To Make a Sallet of a cold Hen or Pullet

from *The Accomplisht Ladys Delight* by Hannah Woolley

Take a Hen and roast it, let it be cold, Carve up the Legs, take the Flesh and mince it small, shred a lemon, a little Parsley and Onions, an Apple, a little Pepper and Salt, with Oyl and Vinegar, garnish the Dish with the bones and Lemon-peel, and so serve it.

Our Version

1 cup (1 breast + 1 thigh) cold cooked chicken, skinned and finely chopped
1 medium apple, finely chopped
1 tablespoon chopped onion or chives
1 tablespoon chopped parsley

DRESSING
⅛ cup lemon juice
2 tablespoons olive oil
1 teaspoon cider vinegar
Salt and pepper, to taste

Prepare the dressing and toss with the remaining ingredients. Serve cold.

Spring Salad

Cleopatra: My salad days,
When I was green in judgement, cold in blood,
To say as I said then!
—Antony and Cleopatra

This salad is a blend of the youngest greens found in herb gardens only during the spring: baby spinach, delicate chervil, cucumber-flavoured burnet, and zesty sorrel picked before its leaves turn tough and bitter. The red sage was probably similar to the Purpurea *variety, known for its aromatic purple leaves. A good mesclun mix of young greens can substitute for the spring greens.*

BEAUTY AND THE BEETS

The lush colour of the red beet made it a favourite garnish for dishes. To those in the know, however, it was more than just a pretty vegetable. In *The Gardeners Labrynth,* Thomas Hill attributes almost magical properties to red beets: they could purge evil humours from the body, help "the smelling," relieve earache and sore gums, grow hair while killing lice and nits, heal blisters and burns, relieve diarrhea, expel tapeworms, open up the liver and spleen, and rid one of shingles. And just in case that wasn't enough, Hill adds that beets can cure the bite of a scorpion.

Other grand Sallet

from *The Accomplisht Cook* by Robert May

All sorts of good herbs, the little leaves of red sage, the smallest leaves of sorrell, and the leaves of parsley picked very small, the youngest and smallest leaves of spinage, some leaves of burnet, the smallest leaves of lettice, white endive and charvel all finely picked, washed, and swung in a strayner or clean napkin, and well drained from the water; then dish it in a clean scowred dish, and about the center, capers, currans, olives, lemons carved and slic't, boild beet roots carved and slic't, and dished round also with good oyl and vinegar.

Our Version

Mesclun mix
Capers
Black olives
Lemons, peeled and sliced
Beets, cooked, peeled, and diced
Olive oil
Balsamic vinegar

Wash the mesclun mix and spin it dry. Arrange it on a platter and then arrange the capers, olives, lemons, and beets on top. Mix the oil and vinegar and drizzle over the salad just before serving.

Lemon Salad

This simple presentation of lemon slices with a little zest and sugar serves as a good counterpoint to fried foods or rich meats.

To make a Sallet of Lemmons

from *The Good Huswifes Jewell* by Thomas Dawson

Cut out slices of the peele of the Lemmons long waies, a quarter of an inche one peece from an other, and then slice the Lemmon very thinne and lay him in a dish crosse, and the peeles about the Lemmons, and scrape a good deale of suger upon them, and so serve them.

LEMON SCENTED

Lemons and other seasonings of the day are referred to in this exchange between the pompous Don Adriano de Armado and the lords who mock him in *Love's Labour's Lost*:

Armado: The armipotent Mars,
of lances the almighty,
Gave Hector a gift—
Dumaine: A gilt nutmeg.
Berowne: A lemon.
Longaville: Stuck with Cloves.
Dumaine: No, cloven.

Lemons studded with cloves, as well as gilded nutmegs, were used for scent and flavouring. Gentility carried them to the theatre as an antidote to the smell of the unwashed crowds.

Our Version

2 lemons
Sugar, to taste

Using a paring knife cut some long, thin strips of peel from the lemons, being careful not to take any of the white part. Cut the tops and bottoms off the lemons so they sit flat on a cutting board, then cut away the white pith.

Slice the lemons crossways, removing any pips, then arrange the slices in the centre of the serving plate and arrange the peel around the edges. Sprinkle with sugar just before serving.

A Salad with Flowers and Cucumbers

With orange nasturtium blossoms and dark green spinach leaves this is a particularly colourful salad. The peppery nasturtiums work well with the cucumbers. Thomas Dawson doesn't specify any particular flowers so feel free to substitute other edible blooms such as calendula, violets, or rose petals.

IN A PICKLE

In Shakespeare's day "pickle" had the same colourful associations with being drunk and getting into trouble as it does today:

Alonso: And Trinculo is reeling ripe.
Where should they
Find this grand liquor that hath
gilded 'em?
How cam'st thou in this pickle?

—The Tempest

To make a Sallet of all kinde of hearbes

from *The Good Huswifes Jewell* by Thomas Dawson

Take your hearbes and picke them very fine into faire water, and pick your flowers by themselvs, and whashe them al cleane, and swing them in a strainer, and when you put them into a dish, mingle them with Cowcumbers or Lemmons payred and sliced, and scrape Suger, and put in vineger and Oyle, and throwe the flowers on the toppe of the sallet, and of every sort of the aforeside things and garnish the dish about with the foresaide thinges, and harde Egges boyled and laide about the dish and upon the sallet.

Our Version

4 cups baby spinach leaves, or other young salad greens
1 cup sliced cucumber
1 lemon, peeled and sliced (optional)
8–12 nasturtium blossoms (or other edible flowers)
3 hard-boiled eggs, quartered

Dressing
¼ cup olive oil
2 tablespoons wine vinegar
1 tablespoon sugar
Salt, to taste

Wash and dry the spinach or salad greens, then arrange them in a serving dish. Arrange the cucumber and lemon slices on top of the greens, then arrange the nasturtium blossoms on top of them and place the quartered eggs around the edge of the dish. Mix together the oil, vinegar, sugar, and salt. Dress the salad immediately before serving.

CUCUMBERS

The Elizabethans enjoyed their cucumbers in much the same way that we do today, peeled and sliced in salads or else pickled. However, the shape we now associate with English cucumbers was achieved in Shakespeare's time by putting the young vegetables into hollow canes to force them to grow long, thin, and straight.

Flesh Days

SWINE ON THE RHINE

Hamlet (to his mother): Nay,
but to live
In the rank sweat of an
enseamed bed,
Stew'd in corruption, honeying
and making love
Over the nasty sty!

—*Hamlet*

In *Dyetary of Helth,* Andrew Boorde's chief complaint against the English pig is not its nutritional value, but its unclean quarters and diet: "[A] swyne is an unclene beest, and dothe lye upon fylthy & stynkynge soyles; and with stercorus matter dyvers tymes doth fede in Englande; yet in Hyghalmen [Germany] and other hygh countres...men doth kepe theyr swyne clene, and doth cause them ones or twyse a daye to swymme in great ryvers, lyke the water of Ryne, which is above Coleyne."

Baked Ham with Prune Sauce

I have a gammon of bacon and two razes of ginger, to be deliver'd as far as Charing-cross.
—1 Henry IV

Elizabethan cooks would have been working with a much saltier ham than is generally available in grocery stores today, hence the instructions for boiling before baking. Boiling would also cook the ham so that it could be enclosed in an elaborate pastry presentation, such as Markham suggests, "in the proportion of a pig's head," without the pastry burning before the meat was cooked. We suggest skipping the crust and serving this ham stuffed with parsley and studded with cloves. If you prefer, omit the stuffing—simply bake and glaze.

A gammon of bacon pie

from *The English Housewife* by Gervase Markham

Take a Gammon of Bacon and only wash it cleane, and then boil it on a soft gentle fire till it be boyled as tender as is possible, ever and anon fleeting it clean, that by all means it may boil white: then take off the swerd, and ferce it very well with all manner of sweet and pleasant fercing herbs: then strow store of pepper over it, and prick it thick with cloves: then lay it into a coffin made of the same proportion, and lay good store of butter round about it, and upon it, and strew pepper upon the butter, that as it melts, the pepper may fall upon the Bacon: then cover it, and make the proportion of a pig's head in past upon it, and then bake it as you bake red deer, or things of the like nature, only the Paste would be of Wheat meal.

Our Version

5–7 pounds partially cooked half ham, suitable for roasting	Whole cloves
	Brown sugar, for glaze (optional)

STUFFING

¼ cup finely chopped shallots	½ cup chopped parsley
2 tablespoons butter	½ teaspoon dried, crumbled sage
2 tablespoons sherry	Bread crumbs

Preheat oven to 325°F. Sauté the shallots in butter and add sherry and then parsley and sage. Mix in enough bread crumbs to bind the stuffing mixture. Using a knife with a long, narrow blade and the handle of a wooden spoon make tunnels in the ham and push the parsley stuffing into the tunnels. Score the fat in a criss-cross pattern and push the whole cloves into the outside of the ham. Place it in a shallow roasting pan, insert a meat thermometer into the thickest part, and bake for 20 minutes per pound, or until the ham reaches an internal temperature of 160°F.

If you want a glaze, during the last 20 minutes of cooking sprinkle a little brown sugar on the outside of the ham.

Serving suggestion: Garnish the ham with dried fruits that have been simmered in white wine to rehydrate them, and serve with prune sauce (recipe follows).

ALL'S SWILL THAT ENDS SWILL

Mrs. Page: Wives may be merry,
and yet honest too:
We do not act that often jest and
laugh;
'Tis old, but true: still swine eats all
the draff.

—*The Merry Wives of Windsor*

On the other hand, Gervase Markham, author of *The English Housewife,* is full of praise for the pig and its capacity to consume household waste: "...he is the Husbandmans best scavenger, and the Huswifes most wholesome sinke, for his foode and living is by that which would else rot in the yard and make it beastly, and breed no good meanure, or being cast downe the ordinary sinke in the house breed noysome smels, corruption, and infection: for from the Husband-man he taketh Pulse, Chaffe, Barne-dust, Mans-ordure, Garbage, and the weeds of his yards; and from the Huswife her Draffe, Swilling, Whey, washing of Tubs and such like..."

To make sauce of dry proins

from *Epulario* by Giovanne de Rosselli

Take Proines and steep them in Claret wine, then take out the stones, and stampe them with a few blanched Almonds, and a toste of bread soked in the wine wherein the Proines were steeped, stampe all this together, tempering them with a little verjuice and other bastard wine, or Sugar which is better, then straine them, and put spice unto them, specially Sinamon.

Our Version

1 cup pitted prunes
1 cup red wine
1 tablespoon cider vinegar
2 tablespoons ground almonds
¼ cup sugar
1 teaspoon ground cinnamon
½ teaspoon ground ginger
¼ cup bread crumbs (optional)

Simmer the prunes in the wine and cider vinegar in a covered saucepan until soft, about 20 minutes. Pour the cooked prunes and wine into a blender and purée. Empty into a bowl, then stir in the almonds, sugar, cinnamon, and ginger. If you prefer a thicker sauce, add enough bread crumbs to reach the desired consistency.

Roast Beef with Mustard

Roasted meats customarily were basted with fats such as suet and butter to keep them moist, then dredged with a layer of seasoning as they turned on the spit. A pan was placed underneath to catch the dripping juices.

Mustard was a popular accompaniment to many meat and fish dishes. It was widely grown in England and made some towns famous, as illustrated in the following quote:

Falstaff: He a good wit? Hang him, baboon! his wit's as thick as Tweksbury mustard, there's no more conceipt in him than is in a mallet.
—2 Henry IV

Cookbooks list a variety of ways to prepare mustard at home, including mingling mustard seeds with vinegar, beer, buttermilk, white wine, claret, or the juice of cherries. Suprisingly, a recipe for Dijon mustard appears in Robert May's The Accomplisht Cook *calling for vinegar, honey, and cinnamon and kept "close covered in little oyster barrels." Instructions are also supplied for baking thick mustard paste in "little loaves or cakes to carry in ones pocket."*

One might have bought prepared mustard as an alternative, but in Delightes for Ladies *Hugh Platt cautions against it, saying, "the mustard we buy from the Chandelers at this day is many times made up with vile and filthy vinegar, such as our stomack would abhorre if we should see it before the mixing thereof with the seeds."*

Here then is Platt's recipe: "It is usuall in Venice to sell the meale of Mustarde in their markets, as we doe floer and meale in England: this meale (ground mustard seed) by the addition of vinegar in two or three diaes becometh exceeding good mustard, but it would bee much stronger and finer, if the huskes or huls wer first divided by searce or boulter, which may easily be done, if you drie your seedes against the fire before

Grumio: ...What say you to a piece of beef and mustard?
Katherine: A dish that I do love to feed upon.
Grumio: Ay, but the mustard is too hot a little.
Katherine: Why then the beef, and let the mustard rest.
Grumio: Nay then I will not, you shall have the mustard,
Or else you get no beef of Grumio.

—*The Taming of the Shrew*

you grinde them. The Dutch iron handmils, or an ordinarie pepper mil may serve for this purpose."

Today mustard can be made easily according to Platt's instructions by using a dry mustard powder such as Keene's. As Platt suggests, mustard is better if made a few hours or even a day before serving.

Our Version

Melted butter, for basting
Prime standing rib roast,
 2 ribs (about 5 pounds)
1 teaspoon salt
1 teaspoon pepper
1 teaspoon dried mustard

SAUCE
2 cups hot beef stock
½ cup red wine (optional)
2–3 tablespoons flour (optional)

Preheat oven to 425°F. Brush melted butter on all the lean surfaces of the meat. Mix together salt, pepper, and mustard, then rub them all over the meat. Place the meat ribs downward in a shallow roasting pan.

Insert a meat thermometer into the thickest part of the meat and calculate the cooking time as follows: 20 minutes at 425°F, then reduce heat to 375°F and cook for 15 minutes per pound for rare or 20 minutes per pound for medium-rare. (For example, a 5-pound roast cooked medium-rare needs 2 hours total cooking time: 20 minutes plus 20 minutes x 5.) The meat is cooked when it reaches an internal temperature of 130°F for rare or 135°F for medium-rare.

When the meat is cooked, put it on a warmed platter and leave it to stand in a warm place while you prepare the "sauce" or gravy. For thin gravy, drain excess fat from the roasting pan, then deglaze it with hot beef stock and wine, if using.

If you prefer a thick gravy, leave a little of the fat in the roasting pan and stir in the flour. Cook while stirring on the stove-top, then pour in the hot stock. Continue stirring until the gravy is slightly thickened.

MUSTARD

- Wine vinegar
- Water
- 2 tablespoons dry mustard powder (such as Keene's)
- Cream (optional)
- Sugar (optional)

Make the mustard a few hours in advance, as the flavour improves with time.

In a small dish, mix equal amounts of wine vinegar and water with the mustard until the desired consistency is reached. If you prefer a smoother-tasting mustard, add a little cream and sugar before serving.

Roast Pork Stuffed with Sage

Gervase Markham gives instructions for roasting a whole pig, including the brain, which forms the basis for the sage-flavoured sauce. We've kept the sage flavouring and used a smaller cut of pork. A few apples substitute for the brain.

Sauce for a Pigge

from *The English Housewife* by Gervase Markham

To make sauce for a Pigge, some take Sage and roast it in the belly of the Pigge, then, boiling Verjuice, Butter and Currants together, take and chop the Sage small, and, mixing the brains of the Pigge with it, put altogether, and so serve it up.

SAINT ANTHONY'S PIGS

Government food inspectors in London were known to confiscate goods deemed to be unfit for sale. They cut the ears of sick or starving pigs to prevent them being resold. In one case the pigs would then fall under the "protection" of the proctors of St. Anthony's Hospital.

With identifying bells dangling from their necks, the pigs were free to roam the local "dunguehills" in search of food. Tossing the pigs scraps could prove risky since the pigs' memories were as great as their appetites. The porkers, spotting someone who had once fed them, would trail behind him or her, squealing for more.

So famous did the pigs become that anyone exhibiting similar behaviour was called a St. Anthony's Pig. Alas, as the pigs grew fat, they were relieved of their freedom and roasted in the ovens of the hospital.

Our Version

Butter
2 sprigs of fresh sage
3 apples, peeled and sliced
2 pounds boneless pork loin or shoulder roast suitable for stuffing
Salt
2 tablespoons cider vinegar
½ cup apple juice
¼ cup currants

Preheat the oven to 350°F. Lightly spread a little butter on the inside of the roasting pan. Chop a few sage leaves (about 1 tablespoon chopped sage) and mix with the apple slices. Put the slices in the roasting pan. Push the other sage leaves into the roast, then sprinkle with a little salt and put it in the oven to cook for about 2 hours, or until the internal temperature reaches 170°F.

Mix the cider vinegar and apple juice in a small saucepan. Bring to a boil, then add the currants. Cover and turn off the heat, but leave the pot on the stove, allowing the currants to slowly absorb the juice.

When the roast is cooked, remove it to a warm platter. Pour the warm apple juice and currant mixture into the pan with the cooked apples and sage. Stir well until the apples are somewhat mashed. Slice the roast and serve with the apple and sage sauce.

Serving suggestion: Excellent with parsnips and cabbage.

KITCHEN DOGS

Because there were no cast iron cookstoves in Elizabethan times, open-hearth cooking prevailed. Meat roasted on spits turned by either young children or dogs specially bred for the job of running on treadmills rigged to pulleys that turned the spits.

Antipholus of Syracuse: ...How chance thou art return'd so soon?
Dromio of Ephesus: Return'd so soon! rather approach'd too late:
The capon burns, the pig falls from the spit;
The clock hath strucken twelve upon the bell:
My mistress made it one upon my cheek:
She is so hot, because the meat is cold:

—The Comedy of Errors

She would have made Hercules have turn'd spit, yea, and have cleft his club to make the fire too.

—Much Ado About Nothing

Lamb Chops with Fennel Seed

Shepherd: God knows thou art a collop of my flesh,
And for thy sake have I shed many a tear.
—1 Henry VI

The term collops *refers to small cuts taken from a larger joint of meat, in this case chops cut across the leg. Fennel seeds lend a distinctive period flavour.*

Other hashes of Scotch Collops

from *The Accomplisht Cook* by Robert May

Cut a leg of mutton into thin slices, as thin as a shilling, cross the grain of the leg, sprinkle them lightly with salt, and fry them with sweet butter, serve them with gravy or juyce of orange, and nutmeg, and run them over with beaten butter, lemon, &tc.

For variety, sometimes season them with coriander seed, or stamped fennil-seed, pepper, and salt; sprinkle them with white wine, then flowerd, fryed and served with juyce of orange, for sauce, with sirrup of rose vinegar or elder vinegar.

IDYLLIC

Shakespeare paints an idyllic portrait of English agriculture and sheep farming in the following quote from the goddess of the rainbow to the goddess of agriculture:

Iris: Ceres, most bounteous lady, thy rich leas
Of wheat, rye, barley, fetches, oates, and pease;
Thy tufty mountains, where live nibbling sheep,
And flat meads thatch'd with stover, them to keep;

—*The Tempest*

Paul Hetnzner, a German justice, paints much the same portrait of the English countryside in his travel journal: "There are many hills without one tree or any spring, which produce a very short and tender grass, and supply plenty of food to sheep; upon these wander numerous flocks extremely white, and whether from the temperature of the air or goodness of the earth, bearing softer and finer fleeces than those of any other country."

Our Version

1 teaspoon fennel seeds
½ teaspoon salt
2 tablespoons flour
¼ teaspoon pepper
3 tablespoons white wine
4 lamb chops cut across the leg, each about ½ inch thick
Butter, for frying
1 lemon or orange, cut into 4 wedges

Using a mortar and pestle crush the fennel seeds with the salt. Place them on a plate with the flour and pepper and mix thoroughly. Sprinkle a little wine on the chops, then lightly coat them with the flour mixture.

Fry the chops in butter for roughly 3 minutes on each side. Serve each chop with a wedge of orange or lemon to squeeze for "sauce."

Serving suggestion: Excellent with herbed lima beans.

NOT SO IDYLLIC

As the price of wool increased, many landowners, realizing that they could make more money from sheep than tenants, took over any lands they could. In addition, former Roman Catholic monastery lands, once used as common grazing grounds, were used as political gifts rewarding loyalty to the crown. Tenant farmers no longer able to make a living migrated to cities in search of work.

OXE MORON

Claudio, boasting of his invitation to dinner, misses the insults intended by the symbols of stupidity—the calf's head, capon, and woodcock.

Claudio: ...he hath bid me to a calve's head and a capon, the which if I do not carve most curiously, say my knife's naught. Shall I not find a woodcock too?

—*Much Ado About Nothing*

Veal and Chicken Casserole

Rice cooked with pistachios, pine nuts, and cinnamon also absorbs the flavour of the meat. The garnish of cinnamon and sugar works surprisingly well to enliven the taste. You'll need a large sauté pan for this stove-top casserole.

First, a dish of Chines of Mutton, Veal, Capon, Pigeons, or other Fowls

from *The Accomplisht Cook* by Robert May

Boil a pound of rice in mutton broth, put to it some blanched chesnuts, pine-apple seeds, almonds or pistaches, being boild thick, put to it some marrow or fresh butter, salt, cinamon and sugar; then cut your veal into small bits or pieces, and break up the fowl; then have a fair dish and set it on the embers, and put some of your rice, and some of your meat, and more of the rice and sugar, and cinamon and pepper over all, and some marrow.

Our Version

4 chicken legs	2 cups arborio rice
4 tablespoons olive oil	½ cup pistachio nuts, shelled
2 tablespoons butter	2 tablespoons pine nuts
1 pound stewing veal	Salt and pepper, to taste
3-½ cups chicken stock	2 cinnamon sticks
½ cup white wine	

GARNISH

¼ cup sugar	1-½ teaspoons ground cinnamon

In a large sauté pan, brown the chicken legs in half of the olive oil and butter. Remove the chicken and keep it warm in an oven set at 200°F. Repeat with the veal and remaining oil and butter. Add the chicken stock and wine to the pan. Add the rice, pistachios, pine nuts, salt, pepper, and cinnamon and simmer for 5 minutes. Return the veal and chicken (as well as any juices) to the pan. Cover and cook over medium heat for 20 to 30 minutes until the rice is soft and the meats are cooked. Sprinkle the sugar and cinnamon over top and serve.

TONGUE 'N' CHEEK

In *The Accomplisht Cook* Robert May devotes an entire chapter to "An hundred and twelve Excellent Wayes for the dresing of Beef." Most recipes are for parts that seem unusual to modern cooks: To boil Oxe Cheeks; To dres Oxe Cheeks in Stofadoe (a slow-cooked Spanish stew); Oxe Cheeks in Sallet; To bake Oxe cheeks in a pasty or pie; To stew Pallets, Lips, and Noses; To roste a Neats [ox] Tongue or Udder.

VEAL REARING TIP

In *500 Pointes of Good Husbandry*, Thomas Tusser advises that any calves born too early in the winter be taken into the house to raise. The woman of the house was instructed to take the calf to the barn to suckle twice a day. Before the calf is returned to the herd, Tusser recommends rubbing it with a steak.

Olives of Veal Rolled with Herbs

Katherine: ...is not veal a calf?
Longaville: A calf, fair lady?
Katherine: No, a fair lord calf.
Longaville: Let's part the word.
Katherine: No, I'll not be your half:
  Take all and wean it, it may prove an ox.
—Love's Labour's Lost

The "olives" in the title of this recipe refer to thin slices of veal, like those used in veal scaloppine.

To rost olives of veale

from *The English Housewife* by Gervase Markham

You shall take a legge of veale and cut the flesh from the bones, and cut it out into thin long slices; then take sweet hearbes and the white parts of scallions, and chop them well together with the yolkes of egges, then rowle it up within the slices of Veale, and so spit them and roast them; then boile verjuice, butter, sugar, cynamon, currants, and sweet herbes together, and, being seasoned with a little salt, serve the Olives up upon that sauce with salt, cast over them.

Our Version

6 thin slices veal
⅔ cup chopped parsley
(or chopped fresh oregano, thyme, or marjoram)
4 green onions, white parts only
2 hard-boiled egg yolks, chopped
1 teaspoon flour
1 tablespoon butter

Sauce
1 tablespoon butter
¼ cup white wine
1 tablespoon sugar
½ teaspoon cinnamon
2 teaspoons cider vinegar
¼ cup currants
Pinch of salt

Using a tenderizing mallet, pound the veal slices as thin as possible. Chop together the parsley and green onions and blend them with the egg yolk and just enough flour to prevent the mixture from running. Spread a spoonful on each strip of veal, then roll up each strip jelly-roll style and secure with toothpicks. Sauté the rolls in a frying pan with melted butter, or brush them with a little olive oil and grill them on the barbecue over medium heat, about 20 minutes or until firm.

Meanwhile, prepare the sauce by melting butter in a small saucepan. Add the wine, sugar, cinnamon, cider vinegar, and currants. Simmer slowly for 5 to 10 minutes until the currants are plump. Add the salt.

Spoon the sauce onto a warm serving platter and arrange the veal rolls on top.

GOOD BEEF

The Duke of Wirtemberg, who visited England in 1592, was moved by the beauty of its cows and oxen, low and heavy, for the most part black and yielding flesh "so tender, as no meate is more desired."

Carbonadoes of Beef with Wine Sauce

Shakespeare borrows a cooking term to create an effective image of deft swordsmanship.

Servant: ...before Corioles; he scotch'd him and notch'd him like a carbinado.
—CORIOLANUS

Smaller pieces of meat grilled over coals were known as carbonadoes. According to Gervase Markham, this technique was "first brought out of France, as appears by the name" and used for "divers kinds according to men's pleasures: for there is no meat either boiled or roasted whatsoever, but may afterwards be broiled, if the master thereof be disposed."

Markham recommends "scotching" or scoring the meat with a knife, then rubbing salt into the cuts and basting with melted butter before cooking over coals. But we prefer May's method, which begins with a red wine marinade.

Carbonadoes of Beef, raw, rosted, or tosted

from *The Accomplisht Cook* by Robert May

Take fat surloin and cut it into steaks half an inch thick, or the fore-rib, sprinkle it with salt, and broil it on the embers on a very temperate fire, and in an hour it will be broild enough; then serve it with gravy, and onions minced and boiled in vinegar and pepper, or juyce or oranges, nutmeg, and gravy, or vinegar and pepper onely, or gravy alone.

Or steep the beef in claret wine, salt, pepper, nutmeg, and broil them as the former, boil up the gravy where it was steeped, and serve it for sauce with beaten butter.

Our Version

1-½ cups red wine
½ teaspoon salt
½ teaspoon black pepper
¼ teaspoon nutmeg
2–4 well-marbled loin steaks, at least ½-inch thick
Olive oil, for grilling

Combine the wine, salt, pepper, and nutmeg in a dish large enough to hold the steaks in one layer. Add the meat, ensuring that it is well covered by the marinade. Cover and refrigerate for at least 2 hours.

While the barbecue is heating, remove the steaks from the marinade and pour the marinade into a saucepan. Cook the marinade over high heat, stirring constantly, until reduced by at least half.

Brush the barbecue grill with a little olive oil to prevent the meat from sticking, then grill the steaks to the desired degree of doneness. Serve the steaks with the cooked marinade on the side.

BAD BEEF

Writers of dietary advice generally agreed that fresh beef was a nourishing food for the Englishman. Beef preserved by salting was moderately tolerable. But when it came to smoked meat, or as Boorde described it, "hanged beef," it was of so little nutritive value that he suggested using the side of beef as an umbrella to stop the rain rather than consuming it.

ork Sausages with Sage

Most sausage recipes call for the forcemeat to be stuffed in casings, then hung in the chimney to smoke. But these little, hand-rolled sausages are made without casings. Well-seasoned with sage, they are ready to be fried and eaten fresh.

Sausages of Pork Otherways

from *The Accomplisht Cook* by Robert May

Mince pork with beef-suet, and mince some sage, and put to it with some pepper, salt, cloves, and mace; make it into ball and keep it for your use, or roll them into little Sausages some four or five inches long as big as your finger; fry six or seven of them and serve them within a dish with vinegar or juyce of orange.

Thus you may do a leg of veal, and put nothing but salt and suet; and being fried serve it with gravey and juyce of orange, or butter and vinegar; and before you fry them flower them. And thus Mutton, or any meat.

Or you may adde sweet herbs or nutmeg: and thus mutton.

PUDDING LANE

In a particularly vivid description from *A Survey of London,* John Stow explains that Red Rose Lane in Billinsgate is "now commonly called Pudding Lane, because the Butchers of Eastecheap have their skalding House for Hogges there, and there puddings with other filth of Beastes, are voided downe that way to theyr dung boates on the Thames."

Our Version

1 pound ground pork	¼ teaspoon ground cloves
¼ teaspoon freshly ground black pepper	¼ teaspoon ground mace
½ teaspoon salt	1 teaspoon dried, crumbled sage
	Oil, for frying

Combine all ingredients except the oil, working with your hands until the texture is even. Fry a small patty to test seasoning. Adjust seasoning if necessary, then shape the meat into finger-sized lengths. Fry in a little oil until brown on the outside and cooked through, about 6 minutes. Makes 18 small sausages.

Serving suggestion: Sprinkle 1 teaspoon of cider vinegar on the sausages before serving, or serve with a sharp relish.

CRIME AND PUNISHMENT

In 1560 diarist Henry Machin described the punishment for a man who tried to sell unfit meat. He "was sett on the pelere and ii grett peses of the measly bacun hangyng over his head, and a wrytyng put up that ii yere a-goo he was ponyssed for the sam offense."

Lamb Meatloaf

Because a leg of mutton is much tougher than a leg of lamb, Elizabethans were instructed to chop up the meat, season it, and put it in a bag to be "tosted" over an open fire. The bag was needed to hold the meat mixture together. Modern-day cooks can easily prepare this recipe with ground lamb shaped into a meatloaf. We chose to ignore the added suet.

To rost a Gygot of Mutton

from *The Good Huswifes Handmaide for the Kitchin* attributed to John Partridge

Cut the flesh of a leg of Mutton, take out the bone, and take the flesh that you cut foorth, and chop it small, and put thereto yokes of Egges, Cloves and Mace, Corrans, Rosemarie, Parsley, Time and some suet, and mingle them altogether, and put them into a bag and sowe it up, and so toste it.

MUTTON CAPER

In this passage from *Twelfth Night* Shakespeare makes a pun on capers, referring both to the dance and to the common condiment for mutton.

Toby: What is thy excellence in a galliard, knight?
Andrew: Faith, I can cut a caper.
Toby: And I can cut the mutton to't.

DINNER DEBATE

Suitable discussion topics and questions for dinner table conversation are suggested in *The Schoolmaster, or Teacher of Table Philosophie,* dated 1576:

1. "Is it good to walk immediately after meate or not?" Answer: There are two "sorts of motions." While "toyle" should be avoided after dinner, a leisurely walk, indoors or outdoors, will reawaken the senses.
2. "Is it good to sleep after meate or not?" Answer: Sleep is not

cont'd on p.55

Our Version

1-½ pounds ground lamb	½ teaspoon ground cloves
1 egg, beaten	½ teaspoon ground mace
¼ cup currants	½ cup fresh parsley, finely chopped
1 teaspoon rosemary, crumbled	

Preheat oven to 325°F. Combine all ingredients, working with your hands to create a uniform consistency. Shape into a loaf or round, then place in a baking tin. Roast in oven for 1 hour.

Serving suggestion: Serve the lamb with a dish of capers, the classic Elizabethan accompaniment to mutton.

wholesome while the stomach is full, because it causes the meat to "bee burned...as bread burneth when the Oven is overheated." It will also cause headaches. Postpone sleeping until the meat has left the stomach.

3. "Why do beames of the Moone cause fleash sooner to putrify then of the Sunne?" Answer: "Putrifaction of fleash is nothing els but a secret dissolution converting the solidity of the flesh into moisture." The moon's warmth is "hidden" and therefore increases moisture. In addition, the moonbeams contain a certain "natural property to create a misty dew" that "corrupts" the flesh lying in it.

In an era when the workings of microbes had not yet been observed through a microscope, the process of decay remained a mystery. Elizabethans were aware that unseen forces were at work, but, in this case, moonbeams were suspected of causing rot.

Roast Lamb with Orange Anchovy Sauce

The combination of anchovies and oranges produces a distinctive but delicious sauce for this roast lamb.

BAR SNACKS

We know that anchovies were a common snack food in Elizabethan times from Falstaff's tavern reckoning in *1 Henry IV:*

Item, A capon	2s	2d
Item, Sauce		4d
Item, Sack, two gallons	5s	8d
Item, Anchovies and sack after supper	2s	6d
Item, Bread		ob

Prince: O monstrous! but one halfpennyworth of bread to this intolerable deal of sack!

To roste a Shoulder of mutton with onions and parsley, and baste it with Oranges

from *The Accomplisht Cook* by Robert May

Stuff it with parsley and onions, or sweet herbs, nutmeg, and salt; and in the rosting of it baste it with the juyce of oranges; save the gravy and clear away the fat, then stew it up with a slice or two of orange and an anchove, without any fat on the gravy, &c.

Our Version

4 oranges, preferably a juice variety such as Valencia
2-½–3 pounds lamb shoulder, deboned and suitable for stuffing
½ cup hot water
1 teaspoon cornstarch (optional)
2–3 anchovy fillets, chopped

STUFFING

1 onion, chopped
1 tablespoon butter
¾ cup chopped parsley
1 teaspoon fresh thyme leaves
Pinch of nutmeg

GARNISH
1 orange, cut in thin slices

Preheat oven to 350°F. Cut the 4 oranges in half and squeeze their juice into a bowl (about 1-¼ cups). Reserve about ½ cup of the juice to finish the sauce; the rest is for basting.

To make the stuffing, cook the onion in butter until soft and translucent, but not brown. Add the parsley, thyme, and nutmeg. Stuff the lamb and sew up the pocket, if necessary. (New Zealand lamb shoulders can often be purchased encased in a net of kitchen twine, which makes them convenient for stuffing without needing to sew up the opening.) Place the lamb in a roasting pan just large enough to accommodate it. Insert a meat thermometer into the thickest part of the meat. Pour a little of the freshly squeezed orange juice over it and put it in the oven.

Roast the lamb for 1-½ to 2 hours or until the meat thermometer registers 170 to 180°F. Baste frequently with the orange juice, adding more juice each time. When the lamb is done, remove it to a warm serving platter and keep warm. Skim the fat from the roasting pan. There should be about 1 cup of roasting juices in the bottom of the pan. If it is too dry you may need to add ½ cup of hot water. If slightly thickened sauce is desired, add the cornstarch to the remaining orange juice. Pour the orange juice into the roasting pan and cook on the stove while stirring to break up any lumps. Add the anchovy fillets, one at a time, and taste. If you prefer a stronger flavour, add more anchovies. Allow the sauce to simmer for a few minutes. Crush the anchovy fillets and remove any lumps.

Carve the lamb and arrange slices on a serving platter. Pour the orange anchovy sauce over the lamb and garnish with orange slices.

Good Roots, Good Worts

VALOUR WITHOUT VICTUALS

The relationship between hunger and courage is observed on the battlefield in *1 Henry VI.* After the French lose a battle to the English, who they had supposed were starving, the Duke of Alencon declares:

Lean raw-bon'd rascals! who would e'er suppose
They had such courage and audacity?

Charles, the dauphin, replies:

Let's leave this town; for they are hare-brain'd slaves,
And hunger will enforce them to be more eager.
Of old I know them; rather with their teeth
The walls they'll tear down than forsake the siege.

YOU SAY POTATO...

Elizabethans were acquainted with three different types of potato: the Jerusalem Artichoke or "Canada Potato," the sweet potato or "Skirrets of Peru," and the white or "Virginia Potato." Of the three, the sweet potato appears most often in period recipes. Its bright orange colour and natural sugars would have appealed to the Elizabethan palate.

A Tart to Provoke Courage

How the devil Luxury, with his fat rump and potato finger, tickles these together!
—Troilus and Cressida

Almost identical versions of this recipe appear in two Elizabethan books: John Partridge's The Good Huswifes Handmaide for the Kitchin *and Thomas Dawson's* The Good Huswifes Jewell. *It is probably one of earliest recipes to use a potato. Although dubbed a "tarte," the instructions do not mention a crust. Instead this root dish is baked over coals between two platters—like a covered casserole dish. Since they're small, we didn't think the sparrow brains would be missed. We do know, however, that sparrows were routinely eaten. Shakespeare even tells us their price in* Troilus and Cressida *when Thersites remarks: "I'll buy nine sparrows for a penny..." One period cookbook advises readers to stew sparrows in ale with onions, parsley, thyme, rosemary, saffron, cloves, mace, and butter.*

To make a tarte that is courage to a man or woman

from *The Good Huswifes Jewell* by Thomas Dawson

Take two Quinces, and two or three Burre rootes, and a potaton, and pare your Potaton, and scrape your rootes and put them into a quart of wine, and let them boyle till they bee tender, put in an ounce of Dates, and when they be boyled tender, Draw them through a strainer, wine and all, and then put in the yolkes of eight Egges, and the braynes of three or foure cocke Sparrowes, and straine them into the other, and a little Rosewater, and seeth them all with suger, Cinamon and Gynger, and Cloves and mace, and put in a little sweet butter, and set it upon a chaffingdish of coles betweene two platters, and so let it boyel till it be something bigge.

Our Version

2 parsnips, peeled and chopped	3 eggs
1 sweet potato, peeled and chopped	¼ cup sugar
1 cup white wine	½ teaspoon cinnamon
2 apples, peeled, cored, and chopped	½ teaspoon ginger
6 dates, pitted and chopped	¼ teaspoon cloves
2 tablespoons butter	½ teaspoon mace

Place the parsnips and potato in a stainless steel or enamel saucepan with the wine and start to cook over medium heat for about 10 minutes.

Add the apple and dates to the saucepan and continue cooking. When the roots are soft (after 30 to 40 minutes), remove from the heat, stir in the butter, and mash.

Preheat oven to 325°F. While the vegetable mixture is cooling, whisk together the eggs, sugar, and spices. Prepare a casserole dish by rubbing the inside with oil or butter.

Incorporate the mashed vegetables into the egg mixture and stir until smooth. Pour into the casserole dish and cover. Bake for approximately 1 hour, or until firm.

FROM FEAST TO FAMINE

Cookbook authors wrote more than recipes. Some, like Hugh Platt, addressed social concerns. Throughout the sixteenth century changes in the economy and social structure, compounded by crop failures and disease, led to the "years of dearth." Many of the poor starved to death both in villages and in big cities like London.

In 1596 Platt, author of *Delightes for Ladies,* penned a tract called *Sundrie New and Artificial Remedies Against Famine.* Platt tells readers how to cope with hunger by making cakes from parsnips and by rolling a small piece of alum in the mouth to go 30 days without food.

As well as blaming dealers for the rising price of grain, he warns the rich of the potential social upheaval that could result from famine: "Yea if we would look more narrowly & pierce more deepely with a sharpe eye into the threats and terrours of these times, though religion could work no charity in us towards others, yet reason, and civill pollicy might prevaile so much with us for ourselves and those which are deere unto us, that we should not stay so long untill our neighbours flames take holde of our owne houses, nor trie the extremeties that hunger, and famine may worke amongst us."

BOWLING WITH TURNIPS

While Shakespeare's version of bowling is comical, for John Stow the emergence of bowling was no laughing matter. For him, it not only heralded the demise of "noble" sports such as archery and jousting, but along with cards and dice was leading youth astray.

Turnips Baked with Cheese

To protest her marriage to Fenton, young Anne tells her mother:

Alas, I had rather be set quick i' th' earth, and bowl'd to death with turnips!
—The Merry Wives of Windsor

Many modern diners share Anne's contempt for the lowly turnip, but this recipe, with its ample cheese, is enjoyed by even avowed turnip-haters.

To make a fried meat of Turneps

from *Epulario* by Giovanne de Rosselli

Rost the Turnops in the embers, or else seethe theme whole, then cut or slice them in peeces as thicke as halfe the hast of a knife, which done, take cheese and cut them in the same form and quantity, but some what thinner, then take Sugar, Pepper, and other spices mingled together, and put them in a pan under the peeces of cheese, as if you would make a crust under the cheese, and on top of them likewise, and over it you shall lay the peeces of Turneps, covering them over with the spices aforesaid, and plenty of good butter, and so you shall doe with the faire cheese and Turneps till the pan bee full, letting them fry the space of a quarter of an houre, or more, like a Tart, and this would be one of your last dishes.

Our Version

6 small white turnips	2 tablespoons melted butter
Olive oil	⅓ cup bread crumbs
1–2 ounces grated cheddar cheese	Parmesan cheese (optional)
¼ cup brown sugar	Salt and pepper, to taste

Preheat oven to 325°F. Wash turnips and place in a roasting pan coated with olive oil. Roast until tender (about 45 minutes). Peel turnips and slice thinly. Butter a small casserole dish and fill with alternating layers of turnip and cheddar cheese. Sprinkle 1 teaspoon of brown sugar over each layer of turnips before adding the layer of cheese. Mix together melted butter, bread crumbs, Parmesan (if using), salt, and pepper and sprinkle over the top of the casserole. Bake for 10 to 15 minutes in the oven.

TURNIP TYPES

Turnips were abundant in Elizabethan times and a staple food of the poor. As John Gerard stated in his *Herball or General Historie of Plantes,* "There be sundry sorts of Turneps, some wild, some of the garden; some with round roots globe fashion, other ovall or peare-fashion; and another sort longish or somewhat like a Radish: and of all these there are sundry varieties, some being great, and some a smaller sort... It groweth in the fields and divers vineyards and hop-gardens in most places of England."

ried Mushrooms

Epulario presents three different preparations for mushrooms in one recipe. We like the second suggestion, with garlic, but have omitted the boiling stage, a precaution intended for fungi collected from the wild. Mushrooms were not farmed at that time because Elizabethans did not understand how they reproduced.

To dresse mushromes

from *Epulario* by Giovanne de Rosselli

Make the Mushromes very cleane, and seeth them with two or three heads of Garlike, and crummes of bread, this is done because naturally they are venomous, then take them up, and let the water runne out of them until they be dry, then fry them in oyle, and when they are fried, cast pepper and other spices on them, in flesh time fry them as aforesaied, You may dresse them another way, make them very cleane, then set them on the fire, putting to them larde and Garlike beaten together, with pepper, you may likewise dresse them with oyle, you may fry them also in a frying pan like a pancake.

MAGIC MUSHROOMS

Initially Elizabethans were reluctant to embrace the mushroom, as it was associated with magical overnight appearances and was avoided even by sheep.

Prospero: ...you demi-puppets that
By moonshine do the green sour ringlets make,
Whereof the ewe not bites; and you whose pastime
Is to make midnight mushrumps...

—*The Tempest*

Those with more conservative appetites not only considered mushrooms to be unwholesome, but "dangerous and hurtful." However, there was no stopping the growing passion for new or exotic dishes, much to the chagrin of the minister Harrison, who observed that people will now eat anything "as if nature had ordained all for the belly."

Our Version

8 ounces mushrooms
3 rashers bacon
2 cloves garlic, minced
Pepper, to taste

Clean and slice the mushrooms. Finely dice the bacon and fry it until brown and crispy. Do not drain the fat. Add the garlic to the pan and stir for a couple of seconds, then add the mushrooms to the frying pan and cook until soft. Add pepper.

Serve on toast.

Herbed Lima Beans

From the instructions to blanch them like almonds—a process that removes the husks or skins—we know that the beans in this recipe must be young lima beans, broad beans, or a similar variety, not the long green beans that are eaten whole.

We used a little table salt instead of the bacon suggested in the original recipe, but you can replace the salt with some chopped ham or a few rashers of bacon, diced and then fried until crispy.

The author also suggests cooking "yong Roses" in a similar fashion, but without the bacon.

BEANS, BELLIES, AND BATHWATER

A man may break a word with you,
sir, and words are but wind:
Ay, and break it in your face so he
break it not behind.

—*The Comedy of Errors*

Then, as now, beans had a reputation for causing flatulence. This much-maligned legume was blamed for producing many unappetizing side effects, including "thick winds" in the belly, "hurtfull fumes in the brain," and "corrupt dreams." However, adding ground beans to bathwater was recommended to anyone "desirous to cleanse the skin of his body."

To make meat of young Beanes with flesh or otherwise

from *Epulario* by Giovanne de Rosselli

Take Beanes and blanch them with hot water like almonds, then set them to boile, and when they are boiled, put to them a little Parsely, and Mints well beaten, and seeth them with salt Beefe or Bacon, let it be somewhat green and it is the better. The like may be done with pease and other fruits when they are greene.

Our Version

1-pound bag frozen lima beans
3 tablespoons finely chopped fresh parsley
2 tablespoons finely chopped fresh mint
1 tablespoon butter
½ teaspoon salt

Put the beans in a saucepan of boiling water and simmer until tender (about 5 minutes). Drain. Add the parsley, mint, butter, and salt.

Serving suggestion: Excellent with lamb.

Cauliflower in Piquant Butter Sauce

Lady Macbeth: My royal lord,
  You do not give the cheer. The feast is sold
  That is not often vouch'd, while 'tis a-making,
  'Tis given with welcome. To feed were best at home;
  From thence, the sauce to meat is ceremony,
  Meeting were bare without it.
—Macbeth

Although Robert May mentions a capon in the title of his recipe, it is actually a description of how to cook cauliflower served with a lemony butter sauce. It just happens to be perfect with poultry, whether roasted or boiled.

THE CHALLENGING CAULIFLOWER

Cauliflower was said to have a more pleasant taste than its cousin the cabbage, and was therefore held with "more regard and respect at good mens tables." But while cabbage was grown with great success in English gardens, raising cauliflower proved more challenging. John Parkinson lamented that not only were cauliflower seeds difficult to obtain, but they had to be sown on beds of manure and transplanted into very rich earth "lest you lose the benefit of your labours."

To boil Capon, or Chicken with Collyflowers in the French Fashion

from *The Accomplisht Cook* by Robert May

Cut off the buds of your flowers, and boil them in milk with a little mace till they be very tender; then take the yolks of two eggs, strain them with a quarter of a pint of sack; then take as much thick butter, being drawn with a little vinegar, and a slic't lemon, brew them together; then take the flowers out of the milk, and put them into the butter and sack: then dish up your capon, being tender boild, upon sippets finely carved, and pour on the sauce, and serve it to the table with a little salt.

Our Version

- 1 cauliflower
- 2-½ cups milk
- 2-½ cups water
- 1 teaspoon mace
- ½ cup sherry
- 2 egg yolks
- ½ cup butter
- 1 teaspoon white vinegar
- 1 lemon, peeled and sliced

Cut the cauliflower into florets about 2 inches long. Mix the milk, water, and mace in a large saucepan and bring to a boil. Add the cauliflower. Cook until tender, about 10 minutes.

Reserve 1 tablespoon of sherry in a small bowl with the egg yolks. Pour the remaining sherry into a separate saucepan with the butter. Heat the sherry and butter for a few minutes. Add the vinegar and lemon slices. Simmer for 5 minutes.

Beat the egg yolks and sherry. Remove the sauce from the heat and whisk in the egg yolk mixture. Drain the cauliflower and put it in a serving bowl. Strain the sauce and drizzle it over the cauliflower.

Artichokes and Asparagus

Both of these vegetables were increasing in popularity during Shakespeare's day. Very few recipes use anything but the artichoke bottoms. The leaves were, at best, used as a garnish, although modern diners will probably want to save them to dip in mayonnaise.

Several recipes mention serving asparagus as a garnish, and Hannah Woolley's instructions to extend the freshness of the tender stalks beyond their short growing season illustrates how well they were relished.

OF FINGERS AND FORKS

Artichokes and asparagus seem particularly apt to serve at a Shakespearean feast, as both are eaten with the fingers. Although used on the continent, the fork did not appear at English tables until late in the period.

In his popular travelogues, Thomas Coryat, one of the bard's peers and a fellow frequenter of the Mermaid Tavern, wrote about the use of forks in Italy. The Italian, he noted, "cannot by any meanes indure to have his dish touched with fingers, seing all mens fingers are not alike cleane."

Although Coryat is sometimes credited with bringing the first fork into England, we know that Queen Elizabeth I was presented with decorative crystal forks many years before his travels. Forks would not catch on as a table tool until later in the period and Coryat was teased by his friends for using them at home.

In Shakespeare's day a reference to a fork suggested a barbed arrow head, or perhaps a two-pronged tool, as in this passage from *King Lear:*

Lear: The bow is bent and drawn; make from the shaft.
Kent: Let it fall, rather though the fork invade
The region of my heart.

To fry Artichoaks

from *The Accomplisht Ladys Delight* by Hannah Woolley

When they are boyled and sliced, fitting for that purpose, you must have your yolks of Eggs beaten with a grated Nutmeg or two; when your Pan is hot you must dip them into the Yolks of Eggs, and charge your Pan; when they are fryed on both sides, pour on drawn Butter; And if you will fry Spanish Potatoes then the Sauce is Butter, Vinegar, Sugar, and Rosewater, these for a need may serve for Second Course Dishes.

To keep Asparagus

from *The Accomplisht Ladys Delight* by Hannah Woolley

Parboyl your Asparagus very little, and put them into clarified butter, cover them with it, and when the butter is cold, cover them with Leather, and about a Month after refresh the butter, melt it and put it on again; then set them under ground, being covered with Leather.

Our Version

ARTICHOKES

6 small artichokes
Water
Lemon juice
2 egg yolks
½ teaspoon nutmeg
Butter

Cut the stems and the tops from the artichokes and remove the tough outside leaves. Boil the artichokes in water with a little lemon juice until tender (about 15 minutes). When slightly cooled, peel off the artichoke leaves. (Reserve them to garnish a salad or to eat separately, if you prefer.) Scoop out the choke with a spoon and discard it.

Mix the egg yolks with nutmeg. If the artichoke bottoms are thick, you may cut them into ½-inch slices. Dip them in the yolk mixture and fry them in butter.

ASPARAGUS

1 bunch fresh asparagus
Water
Melted butter or olive oil
Balsamic vinegar

Snap the bottoms off of the asparagus stalks. Bring a little water to a boil and immerse the asparagus, cooking for 2 or 3 minutes. Drain and dress with a little melted butter or olive oil and a dash of balsamic vinegar.

BRING YOUR OWN KNIFE

Guests were expected to bring their own knives, a custom Apemantus questions in *Timon of Athens:*

Methinks they should invite them without knives:
Good for their meat, and safer for their lives.

Knives were the eating implement of choice, used for cutting one's food, then stabbing it and lifting it to the mouth. Often they were engraved with poems that expressed greeting card–like sentiments, which Shakespeare mocks in *The Merchant of Venice:*

Gratiano: About a hoop of gold, a paltry ring
That she did give me, whose posy was
For all the world like cutler's poetry
Upon a knife, 'Love me, and leave me not.'

WHERE DID YOU GET THAT TURNIP?

Herbalist John Gerard tells us that the small turnips grown in the sandy soil by Hackney and sold in the vegetable market at Cheapside were without a doubt the best he had ever tasted.

We are likewise warned to avoid turnips that flower in the same year that they are sown, as these are "a degenerat kind, called in Chesire-about-the-Namptwitch, Madneps of their evill qualitie in causing frensie and giddinesse of the brain for a season."

Sweet and Sour Turnips

Emilia: ...Let husbands know
Their wives have sense like them; they see, and smell,
And have their palates both for sweet and sour,
As husbands have.
—Othello

The piquant sauce perks up the humble root, making it a fitting accompaniment to any roast.

To hash Rabits, Chickens, or Piegeons, either in pieces, or whole with Turnips

from *The Accomplisht Cook* by Robert May

Boil either the Rabit or fowls in water and salt, or strained oatmeal and salt.

Take Turnips, cut them in slices, and after cut them like small lard an inch long, the quantity of a quart, and put them in a pipkin with a pound of butter, three or four spoonfuls of strong broth, and a quarter of a pint of wine vinegar, some pepper and ginger, sugar and salt; and let them stew leasurely with some mace the space of two hours; being very finely stewed, put them into beaten butter, beaten with cream and yolks of eggs, then serve them upon fine thin toasts of french bread.

Or otherways being stewed as aforesaid without eggs, cream, or butter, serve them as formerly. And these will serve for boiled Chickens, or any kind of Fowl for garnish.

Our Version

- 1 yellow turnip (rutabaga), diced
- ½ cup butter
- 1 cup beef, lamb, or chicken stock
- ¼ cup wine vinegar
- 5 peppercorns
- 1 teaspoon ground ginger
- ½ cup sugar
- 1 teaspoon salt
- 1 teaspoon mace

Put the turnips in a stainless steel or enamel saucepan with the other ingredients. Bring to a boil, then simmer until tender, at least 1 hour. Remove the peppercorns and mash the turnips.

ennel Purée

Although this recipe calls for young shoots only "4 Fingers high," modern cooks will have to make do with a mature fennel bulb. The resulting purée is particularly good when served with lamb.

To make a Sallet of Fennel

from *The Accomplisht Ladys Delight* by Hannah Woolley

Cut your Fennel while it is young, and about 4 Fingers high, tye it up in bunches like Asparagus, gather enough for your Sallet, and put it in when your Water is boyling hot, boyle it soft, drain it, dish it up with Butter as the Green-pease (ie. put in some good sweet Butter, Salt it, and stir it well together, and so serve it.)

Our Version

1 fennel bulb
2 cups chicken stock or water
2 tablespoons butter
Salt, to taste

Clean the fennel and cut it into 2-inch lengths. Bring the stock or water to a full boil and simmer the fennel until it is tender. Purée the cooked fennel in a food processor, adding a little of the cooking liquid if it seems too dry. Season with butter and salt.

FENNEL FOOT SOAK

To some Elizabethans, fennel was a symbol of enticement. Others believed that eating it would improve the sight and drive out stubborn coughs. And still others used it to bathe their feet.

To rid yourself of "vapours and fumes dimming and overcasting the mind," soak your feet in a bath made from bay leaves, rosemary, and fennel.

FENNEL AFOOT

Such comfort as do lusty young men feel
When well-apparell'd April on the heel
Of limping Winter treads, even such delight
Among fresh fennel buds shall you this night
Inherit at my house;
—*Romeo and Juliet*

abbage in Broth

Although this recipe was intended to accompany "powdered" or salted beef, it is a flavourful method of cooking cabbage to serve with any strong-tasting meat. Cooking cabbage in a meaty broth probably elevated the status of this lowly wort, making it seem more palatable to the higher classes.

How to make long worts

from *The Good Huswifes Handmaide for the Kitchin* attributed to John Partridge

Take a good quantitie of Colewortes and seeth them in water whole a good while, then take the fattest of powdered beefe broth, and put to the woortes, and let them seeth a good while after: then put them in a platter and lay your poudred beefe upon it.

Our Version

½ small head cabbage
3 cups beef or lamb stock

Cut the centre out of the cabbage, then cut it lengthwise into wedges and arrange them in a saucepan. Cover with stock and boil for roughly 15 minutes, until tender.

WORT PLAY

Shakespeare plays on words and worts in this passage from *The Merry Wives of Windsor:*

Evans: Pauca verbs, Sir John; goot worts.
Falstaff: Good worts? good cabbage!

POOR CABBAGE

Cabbages were commonly called coleworts. Like turnips, they were looked upon as a poor man's food, although with proper cooking and dressing they might appear at a rich man's table in order to "delight a curious plate," as Parkinson says. He also advises planting them downwind from one's residence so as not to be overwhelmed by their pungent odour.

Beasts for Sport and Table

abbit in Wine Sauce

Rosaline: I pray you do not fall in love with me,
For I am falser than vows made in wine.
—As You Like It

A wine sauce thickened with egg yolks makes this rabbit stew special.

To hash or boil Rabits divers wayes, either in quarters or slices, or cut like small dice, or whole, or minced.

from *The Accomplisht Cook* by Robert May

Take a Rabit being flayed, and wiped clean, cut off the legs, thighs, wings and head, and part the chine into four pieces of six; put all into a dish, and put to it a pint of white wine, as much fair water and gross pepper, slic't ginger, some salt butter, a little time, and other sweet herbs finely minced, and two or three blades of mace; stew it the space of two hours leasurely; and a little before you dish it, take the yolks of six new laid eggs, and dissolve them with some grapes, verjuyce, or wine vinegar, give it a walm or two on the fire, till the broth be somewhat thick; then put it in a clean dish, with salt about the dish, and serve it hot.

TABLE MANNERS

Young diners learned table manners from popular books of etiquette, such as those that Touchstone alludes to in *As You Like It:* "O sir, we quarrel in print, by the book—as you have books for good manners." Much of the advice in these books seems familiar to modern parents:

Don't

Belch in another's face

Slurp your soup

Stuff your mouth with too much food

Pet the cat or dog

Fight at the table

Make faces

Laugh with your mouth full

Put your elbows on the table

Do

Keep your mouth closed while you eat

Wipe your mouth with your napkin

Clean your hands before you eat

Our Version

1 rabbit
Flour
Salt and pepper
Butter
½ cup chopped shallots
¼ cup sherry
3 cups white wine or stock, or a combination of both
6 peppercorns
1-inch piece of peeled ginger root
3 sprigs of thyme
3 sprigs of parsley
2–3 pieces whole mace
3 egg yolks
2 tablespoons cider vinegar

Wash the rabbit in water with a little white vinegar. Cut it into pieces and dredge it in flour seasoned with salt and pepper. Melt the butter in a large skillet or sauté pan and sauté the shallots. Remove the shallots from the pan and sauté the pieces of rabbit. Add the sherry. Cook for 2 to 3 minutes, then add the wine or stock. Tie the peppercorns, ginger root, thyme, parsley, and mace in a piece of cheesecloth and add to the pan. Cover and simmer until the meat is done, about 1 hour. Remove the seasonings, add the shallots, and simmer for another 5 minutes.

Remove the pieces of rabbit and put them on a warm platter while you thicken the sauce. Beat the egg yolks and vinegar with a little of the broth from the pan. Remove the pan from the heat and whisk in the egg mixture. Serve the rabbit covered with the sauce.

Serving suggestion: Serve with fresh bread and a green salad.

Other words of guidance may seem more peculiar:

Don't

Dip your meat in the communal salt-cellar

Gnaw on the bones

Throw bones under the table

Carve up the table with your knife, use it to pick your teeth, or wipe it on the tablecloth

Spit across the table or into your wash basin

Bite into the meat you are sharing with others if you have putrid teeth

Dip your thumb into your drink

Put your knee under the thigh of the person next to you

Do

Watch your spoon to ensure it isn't stolen

(If you must spit) make sure you rub it into the ground with your foot

Roasted Rabbit for King Henry VIII

I knew a wench married in an afternoon as she went to the garden for parsley to stuff a rabbit...
—The Taming of the Shrew

We've added a stuffing suggested by Robert May: "Sage and parsley minced, roul it in a ball with some butter, and fill the belley with this stuffing." Frequent basting with butter is the key to success with this delicious roast rabbit that is truly fit for a king.

ST. BARTHOLOMEW'S DAY FAIR

This fair was so popular that drink and food vendors sometimes ran out of wares before it was over. One of the main events was the appearance of the mayor at the wrestling matches. After the winning fighters received their prizes, a number of live rabbits were let loose into the crowd, where they were chased by young boys.

Fine Sauce for a roasted Rabbet: used to king Henrie the eight

from *The Good Huswifes Handmaide for the Kitchin* attributed to John Partridge

Take a handfull of washed parcelie, minced small, boil it with butter and vergious upon a chafingdish, season it with Sugar, and a litle pepper gose beaten: when it is readie put in a few crums of white bread amongst the others let it boile againe til it be thick: then lay it in a platter, like the bredth of three fingers, lay of each side one rosted Cony or mo, & so serve them.

Our Version

1 rabbit, approximately 2-½ pounds
Flour
Salt
Pepper
Melted butter

STUFFING
½ cup chopped parsley
A few sage leaves, chopped
¼ cup butter, slightly softened

SAUCE
½ cup butter
2 cups finely chopped parsley
½ teaspoon pepper
Juice of ½ lemon
1 tablespoon sugar
2–3 tablespoons bread crumbs

Clean the rabbit by washing it in a basin of water to which 2 or 3 tablespoons of white vinegar have been added. Preheat oven to 400°F.

Make the stuffing by mixing the parsley and sage with the butter. Roll it into a ball and place it in the rabbit, then pin or sew the belly closed. Mix the flour, salt, and pepper. Melt the butter and brush it all over the rabbit, then cover the rabbit with the seasoned flour. Place the rabbit on its side on a rack in a roasting pan and put it in the oven. Reduce the heat to 350°F. Baste with butter every 15 minutes. Turn the rabbit over after cooking for 45 minutes. Cook for about 1-½ hours total until tender.

Five minutes before the rabbit is done, prepare the sauce by melting the butter, then adding the parsley and pepper. Add the lemon juice, sugar, and bread crumbs just before serving. (Do not add the juice any sooner or the parsley will become discoloured.)

To serve, cut the rabbit into 6 to 8 portions and arrange the pieces around the sauce on a warm platter.

Venison with Red Currant Sauce

Venison is an extremely lean meat. We recommend frying a large steak cut from the haunch in butter and oil to brown the outside while keeping the inside rare and moist. For the sauce we suggest a variation of the fruity Cumberland Sauce, which combines the spices suggested in the original recipes.

DEER FOR THE DEAR

Both Elizabeth I and King James I were fond of deer hunting, and the royal parks—all 200 of them—were well stocked. One chronicler of the times remarked that they "contained more fallow Deere then all the Christian World besides."

Deer were also popular presents, either whole or baked in large pies. The Elizabethans were energetic gift givers and known to present each other with such marvels as parrots, monkeys, marmosets, and hawks, as well as the more traditional tokens of wine or a jar of preserves.

To roast Venison

from *The English Housewife* by Gervase Markham

If you will roast any venison, after you have washed it, and cleansed all the blood from it, you shall stick it with cloves all over on the outside; and if it be lean you shall lard it either with mutton lard, or pork lard, but mutton is the best: then spit it and roast it by a soaking fire, then take vinegar, bread crumbs, and some of the gravy which comes from the venison, and boil them well in a dish; then season it with sugar, cinnamon, ginger, and salt, and serve the venison forth upon the sauce when it is roasted enough.

To roste Venison

from *A Proper New Booke of Cookery*

Rosted Venison must have Veniger, Sugar, and Cinnamon, and butter boyled upon a chafing dish with coles, but the sauce may not be to tarte, and then lay the Venison upon the sauce.

Our Version

2–3 pounds venison steak, ¾-inch thick, cut from the haunch	3 tablespoons butter 2 tablespoons oil

Marinade

¼ cup olive oil ¼ cup red wine	Pinch of cloves

Red Currant Sauce

1 lemon ¾ cup red currant jelly 2 cinnamon sticks	1-inch piece of fresh ginger ¼ cup port

Trim any membrane and sinew from the steak and place the meat in a shallow bowl. Beat the marinade ingredients together until they form a thick emulsion, then pour over the venison. Marinate for 2 to 3 hours.

Start the sauce. Cut the lemon in half and squeeze out the juice. Trim about 1 teaspoon of zest from the peel. In a small saucepan combine the lemon juice with the red currant jelly, cinnamon, and ginger. Simmer for 10 minutes.

Melt the butter and oil in a large frying pan and sauté the steak for approximately 5 minutes per side. Venison should be served rare or it will be very tough. Remove the steak to a warm serving platter while you finish the sauce.

Pour the fat out of the frying pan and deglaze the pan with the port. Pour in the jelly mixture. Cook for a minute, then remove the ginger and cinnamon.

Slice the steak as thinly as possible and drizzle sauce over it.

RED-HOT VENISON

Page: I am glad to see your worships well. I thank you for my venison, Master Shallow.
Shallow: Master Page, I am glad to see you. Much good do it your heart! I wish'd your venison better, it was ill kill'd.

—*The Merry Wives of Windsor*

Several biographers have suggested that the young Shakespeare poached deer from a Stratford park or free-warren, running afoul of local authorities.

Fish Days

HERRINGS LIKE HUSBANDS

Clown: No, indeed sir, the Lady Olivia has no folly. She will keep no fool, sir, till she be married, and fools are as like husbands| as pilchers are to herrings, the husband's the bigger.

—Twelfth Night

Herring Pie

Benvolio: Here comes Romeo, here comes Romeo.
Mercutio: Without his roe, like a dried herring: O flesh, flesh, how art thou fishified!
—Romeo and Juliet

Herrings, like most fish, could be bought fresh or preserved. The combination of pickled herrings, red wine, raisins, cinnamon, currants, and sugar may sound bizarre, but the resulting pie is a tasty novelty for adventurous eaters that resembles a fishy version of mincemeat.

A Herring Pie

from *The English Housewife* by Gervase Markham

Take white pickled Herrings of one nights watering, and boil them a little: then pill off the skin, and take only the backs of them, and picke the fish cleane from the bones, then take good store of raysins of the Sunne, and stone them, and put them to the fish: then take a warden or two, and pare it, and slice it in small slices from the chore, and put it likewise to the fish: then with a very sharpe shredding knife shred all as small and fine as may be: then put to it good store of currants, suger, cinamon, slic't dates, and so put it into the coffin with good store of very sweete butter, and so cover it, and leave only a round vent hole on the top of the lid, and so bake it like pies of that nature. When it is sufficiently bak't, draw it out, and take Claret wine and a little verjuice, suger, cinamon, and sweete butter, and boil them together; then put it in at the vent hole, and shake the pie a little, and put it againe into the oven for a little space, and so serve it up, the lid being candied over with suger, and the sides of the dish trimmed with suger.

Our Version

14-oz jar of pickled herring fillets (about 2 cups when drained)
Flaky pie crust for one 9-inch pie (see page 124)
½ cup red wine, preferably Bordeaux style
2 tablespoons butter
⅓ cup sugar
½ teaspoon cinnamon
¼ cup raisins
¼ cup currants
12 pitted dates (about ½ cup)
2 firm pears such as Bosc, peeled, cored, and chopped
Milk
Sugar (optional)

Drain the herring fillets and discard onions and other seasonings. Remove any bones from the fillets and soak them for about 1 hour in cold water. Rinse and put them in a pot with fresh water, then bring it to a boil. In the meantime, roll out the pastry and line the pie plate. Preheat the oven to 375°F.

As soon as the pot of water boils, drain the fillets. If the fillets are soft they may disintegrate as they come to a boil; if they do, drain the pulp and let the water run off through a fine sieve. If the fillets stay together, chop them finely.

Pour the wine, butter, sugar, and cinnamon into a small saucepan and gently bring it to a boil over low heat. Wash and pick through the raisins and currants, slice the dates, and put them in the wine mixture to simmer, about 10 to 15 minutes. Put the chopped pears into a mixing bowl. Add the chopped herring and wine mixture and stir. Place the mixture in the pie shell and cover with pastry lid. Crimp the edges, cut vents, brush with milk, and trim with pastry scraps. If desired, sprinkle a little sugar on top of the crust. Bake in the oven for approximately 45 minutes.

Serving suggestion: Best eaten hot with a salad on the side.

TAKEOUT FOOD

Pies were a popular takeout food, even though their contents were often suspect. They were commonly purchased at cookshops, a London fixture since the twelfth century, where diners could either eat in or take food away. Fare included sheep's feet, mackerel, soup, oysters, ribs of beef, and pies of all descriptions.

Originally located near the docks to serve river traffic, cookshops gradually moved to the inner city to serve a local population too busy to cook for themselves. Every Londoner was familiar with the neighbourhood known as Pie Corner, including Shakespeare, whose Mistress Quickly tells us that Falstaff "comes continually to Pie Corner."

CRIME AND PUNISHMENT

In 1560 a fishmonger was apprehended for stocking young fish too small to meet the official measurement for sale. As punishment she was forced to wear a garland of the illegal fish on her head, put on a horse, and, escorted by police, led through the streets of Cheapside.

Fried Whitings

Clown: Truly, Fortune's displeasure is but sluttish if it smell so strongly as thou speak'st of. I will henceforth eat no fish of Fortune's butt'ring.
—ALL'S WELL THAT ENDS WELL

Whitings, also known as hake, are a common European saltwater fish belonging to the cod family. North American whitings belong to a different family, but this simple method of frying works well for almost any whole, young fish, including sea smelts and trout. If using a larger fish, you can cut fillets instead of frying the whole fish. Frying with a combination of oil and butter gives the fish a nice golden-brown colour without burning it.

You may choose to omit the applesauce and serve the fish simply with lemon wedges.

To fry Whitings

from *A Book of Cookrye* by A.W.

First flay them and wash them clean and scale them, that doon, lap them in floure and fry them in Butter and oyle. Then to serve them, mince apples or onions and fry them, then put them into a vessel with white wine, vergious, salt, pepper, cloves & mace, and boile them togither on the Coles, and serve it upon the Whitings.

Our Version

8 whitings, about 1 pound in total
Oil
Butter
Flour, for dredging

Sauce

1 onion, finely diced
1 tablespoon butter
2 apples, peeled and chopped
½ cup white wine
1 teaspoon cider vinegar
2 cloves
½ teaspoon ground mace
Salt and pepper, to taste

Prepare the sauce first. Sauté onions in butter, then add apples. When the apples begin to soften, add the remaining ingredients and simmer for 10 minutes.

Clean the whitings, removing any scales and guts. Heat oil and butter in a frying pan. Dredge the fish in flour. Fry the fish, for roughly 5 minutes on each side, until golden and crispy. Add more oil and butter as necessary.

Serve the whitings with a spoonful of sauce on the side.

Baked Trout

Th' imperious seas breeds monsters; for the dish,
Poor tributary rivers as sweet fish.
—Cymbeline

This simple recipe produces a moist fish cooked in its own juices. While Elizabethan cooks wrapped the trout in a pie crust, with eels added for their fat, we suggest using buttered foil.

To bake a Trout

from *The Good Huswifes Handmaide for the Kitchin* attributed to John Partridge

Wash it a litle, and take two or three Eeles, a few Cloves, Mace, ginger, and Salt, and season the Trowt and the Eele together, and put them in the coffin together, and a few Corrans about it, and a quantitie of Butter, and let them bake an houre and a halfe.

TICKLISH TROUT

...here comes the trout that must be caught with tickling.

—Twelfth Night

Anglers without hooks, lines, and rods caught fish with their bare hands, a technique known as tickling.

Pompey: Yonder man is carried to prison.
Mrs. Overdone: Well, what has he done?
Pompey: A woman.
Mrs. Overdone: But what's his offense?
Pompey: Groping for trouts in a peculiar river.

—Measure for Measure

Our Version

1 large rainbow trout (about 1-½ pounds)	3 pieces whole mace
Butter	Small slice of fresh ginger
3 whole cloves	Salt, to taste

Preheat the oven to 350°F. Wash and clean the trout, but leave on the head and tail. Butter a sheet of aluminum foil large enough to wrap the fish. Put the cloves, mace, ginger, and salt in the trout's belly, then close up the foil packet. Bake until the flesh is white and opaque (about 40 to 45 minutes).

To serve, peel off the skin by cutting along the gills and down the back to the tail. You should be able to peel the skin off gently, then lift the flesh from the bones.

A PECULIAR FISH BAIT

Hugh Platt's recipe for fish baits, launched in paper boats instead of fastened to hooks, would seem to require the use of one's hands, as in tickling the trout: "To a hotte half penie white loaf, take one ounce of Cocleseed, one ounce of Henbane seed finely powdered, temper the same wel with strong Aqua composita into a past, then divide your past into small peeces, of the bignesse of a graine of wheate, and cast in a handefull of them at once, somewhat above the place where the fish doe haunt, if it be in a river." He closes by adding, "This secret I have not proved."

Poached Salmon with Lemon Butter Sauce

A tangy lemon sauce tops this delicately poached fish. If you prefer to eat it cold without the sauce, do as Robert May suggests: Chill it in the poaching liquid until you are ready to serve it.

HEADS OR TAILS

While thrifty Elizabethans would have dined on a serviceable cod's head, spendthrifts would have splurged for a salmon's tail, as evidenced in this passage from *Othello:*

Iago: ...She that in wisdom never was so frail
To change the cod's head for the salmon's tail...

To calver Salmon to eat hot or cold

from *The Accomplisht Cook* by Robert May

Chine it, and cut each side into two or three pieces according to the bigness, wipe it clean from the blood, and not wash it; then have as much wine and water as you imagine will cover it, make the liquor boil and put in a good handful of salt; when the liquor boils put in the salmon, and boil it up quick with a quart of white wine vinegar, keep up the fire stiff to the last, and being throughly boild, which will be in the space of half an hour or less, then take it off the fire and let it cool, take it up into broad bottomed earthen pans, and being quite cold, which will be in a day, a night, or twelve hours, then put in the liquor to it, and so keep it.

Some will boil in the liquor some rosemary bound up in a bundle hard, two or three cloves, two races of slic't ginger, three or four blades of large mace, and a lemon-peel. Others will boil it in beer onely.

Or you may serve it hot, and dish it on sippets in a clean scowered dish; dish it round the dish or in pieces, and garnish it with slic't ginger, large mace, a clove or two, gooseberries, grapes, barberries, slic't lemon, fryed parsley, ellicksanders, sage, or spinage fryed.

To make sauce for the foresaid salmon; beat some butter up thick with a little fair water, put two or three yolks of eggs dissolved into it, with a little of the liquor, grated nutmeg, and slome slic't lemon, pour it on the salmon, and garnish the dish with fine searsed manchet, barberries, slic't lemon, some spices, and fryed greens as aforesaid.

Our Version

4 salmon fillets, or salmon steaks, approximately 1 inch thick
1 cup white wine
2 cups water
1 teaspoon salt
1 tablespoon white vinegar

SAUCE
3 tablespoons butter
½ cup poaching liquid
2 egg yolks
Juice of ½ lemon
¼ teaspoon nutmeg

GARNISH
Lemon slices
Parsley

Use a covered saucepan large enough to hold all of the salmon fillets in one layer. Pour in white wine and water, deep enough to cover the salmon. Add salt and vinegar. Bring to a boil, then add the salmon. Cook until the flesh is cooked through but still moist and tender (about 10 minutes).

Remove the fish from the saucepan to a warm serving dish and make the sauce. In a small saucepan, melt the butter and add the poaching liquid. Beat the egg yolks with the lemon juice and whisk it into the butter mixture. Add the nutmeg. Cook gently until slightly thickened. Drizzle on the salmon fillets.

Garnish each fillet with lemon slices and parsley. To be truly authentic you can fry the parsley first.

Serving suggestion: An excellent springtime meal when served with asparagus.

TO BAIT A KING

A man may fish with the worm that hath eat of a king, and eat of the fish that hath fed of that worm.

—Hamlet

Boiled Mussels

I'll manacle thy neck and feet together.
Sea-water shalt thou drink; thy food shall be
The fresh-brook mussels, wither'd roots, and husks
Wherein the acorn cradled.
—The Tempest

This simple method for cooking mussels is still a classic. Some Elizabethan cooks saved the empty mussel shells to use as molds when baking small cakes.

To boile Muskles

from *The Good Huswifes Jewell* by Thomas Dawson

Take water and yest and a good dish of butter, and Onions chopt, and a lyttle pepper, & when it hath boyled a litle while, then see that your Muskels bee cleane washed, then put them into the broth shels and all, and when they be boiled wel, then serve them broth and all.

FISHMONGERS

In addition to oysters, mussels, and cockles, shoppers could buy both fresh and preserved fish from the large London fish market near Queenhythe. The Duke of Wirtemberg, who visited the market in 1592, wrote: "They sell also cod, plaice, small white river fish, pike, carp, trout, lobster and crawfish, and in fine all kinds of sea fish which are sold like meats in other parts both fresh and salted."

Freshwater fish such as pike, trout, tench, and eel arrived from local rivers, streams, and the large fishponds maintained on country estates that also employed their own anglers.

The Fishmongers Company, incorporated in 1536 and one of the largest trade guilds, was originally two separate entities. Sale of dried fish, such as cod or haddock from northern waters, was first controlled by the Stockfishmongers. Another company, the Saltfishmongers, dealt in pickled or salted fish, including whiting, mackerel, pilchard, and the herring that was a popular export to Spain and Italy.

Our Version

2 pounds mussels	1 small onion, thinly sliced
¾ cup white wine	¼ teaspoon pepper
½ cup water	2 tablespoons butter

Clean the mussels thoroughly. Trim off the beards (shaggy-looking undigested bits of seaweed) and discard any mussels that don't shut tightly.

Put the wine, water, onion, pepper, and butter in a covered pan large enough to hold the mussels. Bring this mixture to a boil, then add the mussels. Cook until the mussels are open and opaque (about 10 minutes). Serve in soup bowls with cooking juices.

Serving suggestion: A fresh loaf of white bread to sop up the juices and butter are all that are needed to complete this delicious meal.

Broiled Oysters

Fool: Canst tell how an oyster makes his shell?
Lear: No.
Fool: Not I neither; but I can tell why a snail has a house.
Lear: Why?
Fool: Why, to put 's head in, not to give away to his daughters, and leave his horns without a case.
—King Lear

Atlantic oysters were so plentiful in Elizabethan England that cooks often used them in ways that seem cavalier to us: as stuffing for a leg of lamb or chopped up with other fish in a pie. The following treatment maintains the oyster's inherent flavour and texture.

OYSTER OPENING TIP

If you have difficulty using an oyster knife, you can broil the oysters to open them, as May suggests, or steam the oysters open, using a minimal amount of liquid. You have to work quickly to avoid overcooking these delicate shellfish, so only steam three or four at a time. Put ¼ inch of water in a covered pan, bring it to a boil, and add the oysters. Steam them for 1 or 2 minutes. The shells will not open completely, but will loosen just enough for you to insert a sturdy paring knife and twist open the shell, as Pistol says in *The Merry Wives of Windsor:*

Why then the world's mine oyster,
Which I with sword will open.

To stew Oysters otherways

from *The Accomplisht Cook* by Robert May

Broil great oysters in their shells brown and dry, but burn them not, then take them out and put them in a pipkin, with some good sweet butter, the juyce of two or three oranges, a little pepper and grated nutmeg, give them a walm, and dish them in a fair scowred dish with carved sippets, and garnish it with dryed, grated, searsed fine manchet.

Our Version

12 large oysters	Pepper, to taste
1 cup bread crumbs	Nutmeg, to taste
⅓ cup melted butter	1 orange or lemon, cut in half

Scrub the oysters well with a stiff-bristled brush. Using an oyster knife and oven mitts to protect your hands, open each shell and gently cut the oyster away from the shell. Clean 12 of the best cup-shaped shells and arrange them on a baking tray. Place the oysters in the shells. Preheat the broiler.

Mix the bread crumbs with the melted butter, pepper, and nutmeg. Squeeze a little orange or lemon juice onto the oysters, then sprinkle a little of the buttered crumb mixture on each oyster. Place under the broiler just long enough to toast the crumb topping. Serve immediately.

ARIEL'S SONG

Full fadom five thy father lies,
Of his bones are coral made:
Those are pearls that were his eyes:
Nothing of him that doth fade,
But doth suffer a sea-change
Into something rich and strange.
Sea-nymphs hourly ring his knell:
Burden: Ding-dong.
Hark! now I hear them—Ding-dong bell.

—*The Tempest*

A PEARL OF AN OYSTER

The reputation of the English oyster extended beyond its shores. Supposedly it was sold in the streets of Rome, "being more plentiful and savorie than in any other part."

The oysters' pearls, however, were less esteemed, according to one author: "In the oyster groweth naturali orient perles that oftentimes laye on the see stronde, & be but lytell regarded." The same writer tells us of the curious way that crayfish capture their oyster prey: "whan the oyster gapeth, he throweth lytell stones in him, and so geteth his fishe out."

Sautéed Scallops

These simple but elegant scallops are our favourite seafood dish. Large scallop shells make ideal dishes for individual servings, but you can also use any ovenproof, saucer-shaped dish.

FISH DAYS

Although the royal court issued a proclamation against the eating of flesh on designated "fish days" (Wednesdays and Fridays), licences to exempt oneself from a fishy diet could be had for a price. Payment was made to the parish poor man's box. The other exemption was a medical need for meat. This needed to be substantiated by one's clergyman or physician.

Marine mammals were considered to be fish. Dawson describes how "To bake porpose or Seale" seasoned with salt and pepper, then served with a Gallentine sauce, a dish considered suitable for a Friday dinner.

cont'd on p. 99

To boyl Scollops

from *The Accomplisht Ladys Delight* by Hannah Woolley

First boyl the Scollops, then take them out of the shells, and wash them, then slice them, and season them with Nutmeg, Ginger, and Cinamon, and put them into the bottom of your Shells again, with a little Butter, White-wine, vinegar, and grated Bread, let them be boyled on both sides; if they are sharp they must have Sugar added to them, for the fish is luscious, and sweet naturally; therefore you may boyl them with Oyster Liquor and Gravy, with dissolved Anchovies, minced Onions and Thyme, with the juice of Lemon in it.

Our Version

1 shallot, finely chopped (about ¼ cup)	½ teaspoon vinegar
2 tablespoons butter	1 anchovy fillet
¼ teaspoon thyme	½ cup white wine
	1 pound scallops

TOPPING

2 tablespoons melted butter	Pinch of ginger
½ cup bread crumbs	Pinch of cinnamon
Pinch of nutmeg	

Make the topping by mixing melted butter, bread crumbs, nutmeg, ginger and cinnamon. Preheat the broiler.

In a frying pan, sauté the shallot in butter until translucent. Add the thyme, vinegar, and anchovy. Stir until the anchovy is dissolved. Add the wine and simmer for a couple of minutes. If the scallops are thick, slice them crosswise. Add the scallops to the pan and cook quickly for about 4 minutes until they are no longer translucent, but be careful not to overcook. Divide the scallops and the pan juices between 4 individual ovenproof dishes. Sprinkle topping over each dish. Put the dishes under the broiler until the crumbs are toasted golden-brown. Serve hot.

Serving suggestion: Fresh bread and a salad make this an elegant meal.

Tavern keepers did not always comply with the fish-days statute, as evidenced by this exchange from *2 Henry IV:*

Falstaff: ...Marry, there is another indictment upon thee, for suffering flesh to be eaten in thy house, contrary to the law, for the which I think thou wilt howl.

Mistress Quickly: All vict'lers do so. What's a joint of mutton or two in a whole Lent?

The penalities for non-compliance were stiff: a fine, imprisonment, or the pillory.

el Pie

We combined elements from two of John Murrell's eel recipes, including one taken from a chapter dedicated to London's slightly more sophisticated culinary styles, in our version of a traditional English eel pie.

SLIPPERY EELS

Eels are notoriously difficult to kill and continue to wiggle long after they have been cut into pieces, something Shakespeare must have known when he wrote the following:

Lear: O me, my heart! my rising heart! But down!
Fool: Cry to it, nuncle, as the cockney did to the eels when she put 'em i' th' paste alive; she knapp'd 'em o' th' coxcombs with a stick, and cried, "Down, wantons, down!" 'Twas her brother that, in pure kindness to his horse, butter'd his hay.

—King Lear

To congar Eeles, in collars, like Brawne

from *A New Booke of Cookerie* by John Murrell

Cut them open with the skinne on, and take the bone cleane out, large Mace, gosse Pepper, some fine sweet Hearbs, chopt under your knife. Then straw the Hearbes and the Spices, all along the inside of your Eele, and rowle it like a collar of Brawne: so may you doe with Tenches, boyled in fayre water, white Wine, and a quantitie of Salt, so put in some sliced Ginger, Nutmeg, and Pepper in graine. When it is well boyled put it into an earthen Pan, covered with theyr owne liquour, and a little white Wine-vinegar.

Our Version

1 large eel (at least 3 pounds)
2 shallots, chopped (about ½ cup)
Butter, for frying
½ cup sherry
½ teaspoon each salt, pepper, and nutmeg
Fish stock made with eels (see below)
3 tablespoons butter
4 tablespoons flour
Juice of 1 lemon
½ cup finely chopped parsley
4 hard-boiled eggs (optional)
½ pound puff pastry

STOCK

Eel head and bones	4 peppercorns
Water, to cover	2 cloves
3 bay leaves	½ cup white wine

Ensure that the eels are cleaned well and that the skin and bones are removed. Cut the flesh into 2-inch pieces. Make the stock by cooking the eel head and bones in water with bay leaves, peppercorns, cloves, and wine for 20 minutes.

Sauté the shallots in butter. Add sherry, salt, pepper, and nutmeg. Stir, then add eel pieces. Cover with hot stock. Simmer for 2 minutes. Remove eel pieces and set aside in a warm, deep pie dish or casserole. Preheat oven to 400°F.

Make a *beurre manie* by mixing the 3 tablespoons of butter with the flour, then rubbing the mixture with your fingers until completely blended. Add the *beurre manie* to the stock, then simmer and stir well until thickened. You may need to whisk the sauce to dissolve completely. Add lemon juice and parsley. Pour the sauce over the eel pieces in the pie dish. If using, slice the hard-boiled eggs and arrange the slices on top of the fish.

Roll out a circle of puff pastry to fit the dish and bake until the top is golden, about 40 minutes. After 15 minutes of cooking you may need to turn down the heat to 350°F and cover the pastry with foil to prevent burning.

Serving suggestion: This pie can be eaten hot with rice or bread to soak up its juice or cold when it will have jellied.

EEL EAR OIL

To cure deafness one writer instructs his readers to take a grey eel with a white belly, shove it into an earthen pot, and close the lid tight. Bury the pot in horse manure and let it sit for 20 days. Afterwards, dig up the pot, open it, skim off the freshly formed eel oil, and drop the oil into the affected ear.

EEL BOATS

In Shakespeare's day eel boats plied the Thames River in London, catching an abundance of the long, fatty fish that were often roasted with other species, jellied, or served in pies. Although eels have largely fallen out of favour with modern-day cooks, they are an abundant species and are best bought live; many Asian fish markets carry them. Skinning them is a difficult job, so ask the fishmonger to skin and fillet them for you.

Fine Fowl

hicken Pie with Prunes

Falstaff: There's no more faith in thee than in a stew'd prune...
—1 Henry IV

Both of these original recipes use prunes to enrich the flavour of pie with similar results. We recommend a simplified version made with boneless chicken breasts under a single crust.

To bake Chickins

from *A Book of Cookrye* by A.W.

Season them with cloves, mace, sinamon, ginger, and some pepper, so put them into your coffin, and put therto corance dates Prunes, and sweet Butter, or els Marow, and when they be halfe baked, put in some sirup of vergius, and some sugar, shake them togither and set them into the oven again.

Bake Sparowes, Larkes, or any kind of small birds, calves feet or sheepes tunges after the same manner.

How to bake Conies, Rabets, or Hares, with fruit or without fruit.

from *A Book of Cookrye* by A.W.

Season them with pepper and salt, Cloves and mace, and so lay them into your paste with Corance or Prunes, great Raisins and if you will: butter and a little vergious.

IS THAT A CHICKEN IN YOUR POCKET OR ARE YOU JUST GLAD TO SEE ME?

This Elizabethan joke is adapted from *The Schoolmaster, or Teacher of Philosophy*. It is just one of a collection of the "merie jests and delectable devices" meant to amuse one's dinner guests and prove Shakespeare's contention that "Great men may jest with a saint."

One day King Phillip of France invited some poor priests to dinner. During the meal he noticed the priest at the farthest end of the table take an entire capon and stuff it into the pocket of his robe. After dinner, the king called him aside and asked him what he studied. The priest answered: "Divinity." "Why," said the King, "is it not written in the scriptures that you should not be careful for meat for tomorrow?" "Exactly," said the priest, "and because I was not careful I got caught with this capon."

Our Version

- ⅓ cup sherry
- 20 prunes
- 3–4 boneless, skinless chicken breasts (about 1-½ pounds total)
- 2 tablespoons flour
- ½ teaspoon pepper
- ½ teaspoon ground cloves
- ½ teaspoon ground ginger
- 1 teaspoon salt
- 2 cups sliced onion (about 2 medium onions)
- ¼ cup butter
- Flaky pastry (see page 124)

Put the sherry in a small covered saucepan and bring it to a boil. Add the prunes, turn off the heat, and cover the pan. Preheat the oven to 350°F.

Cut the chicken breasts into pieces no bigger than 1 inch. Mix the flour with the pepper, cloves, ginger, and salt. Dredge the chicken pieces in the flour mixture.

In a large frying pan, cook the onion in the butter until it is translucent but not brown. Add the chicken and cook for 3 or 4 minutes, then add the prunes and sherry.

Put the chicken and prune mixture into a casserole or deep pie dish. Roll out a pastry crust to fit the dish. Cut vents for steam. Bake in the oven for 35 minutes.

A CUPFUL OF COURAGE

Mimicking the dietaries of the day, Falstaff outlines the "nutritive" qualities of his favourite beverage in 2 Henry IV:

...A good sherris-sack hath a twofold operation in it. It ascends me into the brain, dries me there all the foolish and dull and crudy vapors which environ it, makes it apprehensive, quick, forgetive, full of nimble, fiery, and delectable shapes, which deliver'd o'er to the voice, the tongue, which is the birth, becomes excellent wit. The second property of your excellent sherris is the warming of the blood, which before (cold and settled) left the liver white and pale, which is the badge of pusillanimity and cowardice; but the sherris warms it, and makes it course from the inwards to the parts' extremes. It illumineth the face, which as a beacon gives warning to all the rest of this little kingdom, man, to arm, and then the vital commoners and inland petty spirits muster me all to their captain, the heart, who great and puff'd up with this retinue, doth any deed of courage, and this valour comes of sherris. So that skill in the weapon is nothing without sack (for that sets it a-work) and learning a mere hoard of gold kept by a devil, till sacks commences it and sets it in act and use.

Roast Duck in Wine Sauce

She once being loof'd,
The noble ruin of her magic, Antony,
Claps on his sea-wing, and (like a doting mallard),
Leaving the fight in heighth, flies after her.
—Antony and Cleopatra

Use a full-bodied red wine to make this duck finished in a rich wine sauce.

To boil all manner of small Sea or Land Fowls. Otherways

from *The Accomplisht Cook* by Robert May

Take them and roste them, save the gravy, and being rosted put them in a pipkin, with the gravy, some slic't onions, ginger, cloves, pepper, salt, grated bread, claret wine, currans, capers, mace, barberries, and sugar, serve them on fine sippets, and run them over with beaten butter, slic't lemon, and lemon-peel; sometimes for change use stewed oysters or cockles.

POULTRY PRESENTATION

Cooks were expected to dress their meats in a variety of decorative, even fantastical, ways before bringing them to the table. *A Book of Cookrye* suggests that a roast pheasant be presented with one of its feathers stuck in its breast. A roast crane should be carried to the table "With his legs turned up behind him, his wings cut of at the joynt next the bodye, and then winde the neck about the broche, and put the bil into his brest."

Perhaps the most elaborate presentation consists of arranging a cooked chicken in the form of a splayed eagle, a common heralidic symbol. According to Thomas Dawson's instructions, the chicken's bones are broken and the flesh and beak are removed, all without cutting off the head or feet and doing minimal damage to the skin. Before serving, the cooked, minced meat is returned to the bird's empty skin. Then the cook is instructed to arrange the bird "flat in a platter, and make it after the proportion of an Eagle in every part, having his head to be cleft a sunder, and laide in two partes like an Eagles head."

Our Version

1 duck (about 5 pounds)	Salt and pepper

SAUCE

1 onion, sliced
1 cup red wine
½ teaspoon ground ginger
½ teaspoon ground cloves
¼ cup currants
1 cup cranberry sauce
1 cup stock (commercial chicken stock or stock made with the duck neck and giblets)
2 tablespoons sugar

GARNISH

1 lemon, cut into wedges

Preheat the oven to 400°F. Fry the onions until brown and crispy, then drain and set aside. Prick the skin of the duck all over with a fork to release the fat while cooking. Sprinkle the duck with salt and pepper. Place it breast side down on a rack in a roasting pan. Reduce the heat to 350°F. Roast for 30 minutes, turn the duck breast side up, and roast for another 30 minutes. Skim off the excess fat. Remove the duck from the pan and drain any juices into a bowl and reserve. Cut the duck into 4 pieces: 2 breasts and 2 legs. Place the portions in a warm, clean casserole.

Pour the fat out of the roasting pan, then deglaze the pan with red wine. Add the ginger, cloves, currants, cranberry sauce, stock and reserved juices, a few of the fried onions, and sugar. Pour the wine sauce over the duck pieces in the casserole and return to the oven for another 20 minutes. Serve garnished with lemon wedges and the remaining fried onions.

Roast Goose with Apple Gravy

Mercutio: Thy wit is a very bitter sweeting, it is a most sharp sauce.
Romeo: And is it not then well serv'd in to a sweet goose?
—ROMEO AND JULIET

Apples such as the sweetings mentioned in the above quotation are commonly used to counter the gamy flavour of wild birds. While our domestic geese don't have that gamy taste, the apples and other piquant flavours complement the rich, dark goose meat. Besides geese, Elizabethans dined on a wide range of waterfowl, including swans, herons, bitterns, cranes, gulls, and many species of wild ducks. These were served with a galantine sauce of blood and vinegar.

GREEN GEESE AND STUBBLE GEESE

The spring is near, when green geese are-a-breeding.

—*Love's Labour's Lost*

This is the liver-vein which makes flesh a deity,
A green goose a goddess; pure pure idolatry.

—*Love's Labour's Lost*

Green geese were young birds (usually under six months) raised in the spring, and stubble geese were those fattened on the stubble left in the fields after harvest.

Sauces for a Stubble or fat Goose

from *The Accomplisht Cook* by Robert May

1. The goose being scalded, drawn, and trust, put a handful of salt in the belly of it, roast it, and make sauce with sowre apples slic't, and boild in beer all to mash; then put to it sugar and beaten butter. Sometimes for variety adde barberries and the gravy of the fowl.
2. Roast sowre apples or pippins, strain them, and put to them vinegar, sugar, gravy, barberries, grated bread, beaten cinamon, mustard, and boild onions strained and put to it.

Our Version

1 goose, neck and giblets reserved
Salt
1 apple, peeled and quartered
1 onion, peeled and quartered
3 cups water
Peppercorns
1 cup applesauce
1 tablespoon wine vinegar
1 teaspoon ground cinnamon
Pinch of dry mustard
Dried cranberries (optional)

Preheat the oven to 350°F. Wash the goose and remove any remaining quills with pliers. Pat dry and sprinkle salt both outside and inside the cavity. Place the apple and 2 of the onion quarters in the cavity of the goose. Calculate the roasting time (25 minutes per pound) and put the goose on a rack in a roasting pan in the oven.

While the goose is cooking, make stock by boiling the goose neck and giblets in water with a few peppercorns and the remaining onion quarters for about 40 minutes.

Remove goose from the oven when cooked. Pour off the excess fat. (The fat is traditionally reserved for flavouring cabbage and other foods.)

Deglaze the roasting pan with the goose stock (there should be about 1-½ cups). Stir in the applesauce, wine vinegar, cinnamon, mustard, and a few dried cranberries (if using).

POULTRY PUT-DOWNS

Martius: You souls of geese,
That bear the shapes of men, how have you run
From slaves that apes would beat!

—*Coriolanus*

Calling someone the soul of a goose has a regal tone lacking in "scaredy-cat" or "chicken." Here is a fresh batch of Shakesperean insults to invoke when someone incurs your wrath.

Thou damn'd tripe-visaged rascal

Stale old mouse-eaten dry cheese

Stuff'd cloak-bag of guts

Roasted Manningtree ox with the pudding in his belly

Damn'd Epicurean rascal

Cobloaf [misshapen bread]

Bacon-fed knaves

You starveling, you eel-skin, you dried neat's tongue, you bull's pizzle, you stock-fish!

oast Chicken with Garlic Sauce

Prince: What a devil hast thou to do with the time of day?
unless hours were cups of sack, and minutes capons....
—1 Henry IV

Redolent of fresh garlic, the thick and delicious sauce is a powerful accompaniment to almost any meat—roasted or boiled. We've paired it with roast chicken, but if you substitute beef stock for the chicken stock, this sauce would work well with a red meat.

To make good garlike sauce

from *Epulario* by Giovanne de Rosselli

Take blanched Almonds well stamped, and being half beaten, put as much Garlike to them a you thinke good, and stampe them together, tempering them with water least it bee oiley, then take crummes of white bread what quantity you will, and soke it either in lean broth of flesh or fish as time serveth: this sauce you may keepe & use with all meats, fat or leane as you thinke good.

TESTING FOR DONENESS

When roasting meat without the benefit of a meat thermometer, cooks rely on their senses. Gervase Markham deals with the subject by warning that "too much rareness is unwholesome, so too much dryness is not nourishing. Therefore to know when it is in the perfect height, and is neither too moist nor too dry, you shall observe these signs in your large joints of meat; when the steam or smoke of the meat ascendeth, either upright or else goeth from the fire, when it beginneth a little to shrink from the spit, or when the gravy which droppeth from it is clear without bloodiness, then is the meat enough."

Our Version

1 roasting chicken (about 4 pounds)
Salt and pepper, to taste
4–5 garlic cloves
Butter

Sauce
1 cup blanched almonds
6 garlic cloves
1-¼ cup chicken stock
¼ cup fine white bread crumbs
Salt, to taste

Preheat oven to 375°F. Wash the chicken, sprinkle salt in the cavity of the bird, and place garlic cloves in the cavity. Rub a little salt and pepper on the outside of the bird, place it in a roasting pan, and dot a little butter on the breasts. Calculate roasting time (approximately 20 minutes per pound) and put pan in the oven. Baste every 20 minutes. The bird is done when the leg joint moves easily and the juices run clear from the thickest part of the thigh when pricked with a skewer.

While the chicken is roasting, prepare the garlic sauce. Purée almonds, garlic, and chicken stock in blender. Simmer mixture over low heat and stir in bread crumbs. Add salt to taste. Serve garlic sauce in a separate dish alongside the chicken.

Spiced Roast Chicken with Apples and Currants

A rich blend of spices enlivens this simple roast chicken. Elizabethans may have cooked the bird in a pastry coffin, but the recipe works well in a roasting pan. The combination of apples and dried fruits is most commonly seen with fatty birds, like geese or ducks, but it also works well with this chicken dish. The currants plump up with the cooking juices and the apples soften to make a sauce.

To bake chickins

from *The Good Huswifes Jewell* by Thomas Dawson

First season them with cloves & mace, pepper and salt, and put to them currans and Barberies, and slitte an apple and cast synamon and suger upon the apple, and lay it in the bottome, and to it put a dish of butter, and when it is almost enough baked, put a little suger, vergious and orenges.

A CRAVING FOR CURRANTS

Currants helped satisfy an Elizabethan desire for sweetness. The modern cook will be taken aback by the sheer number of period recipes for meat and fish dishes that call for their addition. In fact, the use of currants was so prevalent that one writer was lead to remark: "And the same delight in sweetness hath made the use of Corrands so frequent in all places, and with all persons in England, as the very Greekes that sell them wonder what we doe with such quantities thereof, and know not how we should spend them, except we use them for dying or to feede Hogges."

Our Version

Butter or oil	
1 roasting chicken (about 3–5 pounds)	½ teaspoon cider vinegar (optional)
Juice of ½ orange	1–2 oranges, for garnish (optional)

Seasoning

½ teaspoon ground cloves	½ teaspoon ground pepper
½ teaspoon ground mace	1 teaspoon salt

Stuffing

2 apples, peeled, cored, and sliced	½ cup sugar
½ cup dried currants, washed	1 teaspoon cinnamon

Preheat the oven to 325°F. Prepare a roasting pan with a light coating of butter or oil. Combine the stuffing ingredients and put half of the mixture in the roasting pan. Wash the chicken and put it in the pan, on top of the apple mixture. Put the remaining mixture inside the bird. Do not truss, but tuck the wings behind the bird's back. Combine the seasonings and rub all over the bird's skin. Dot the breasts with butter. Bake the chicken until the leg joints move easily and the juices run clear (approximately 25 minutes per pound).

Let the bird rest for about 10 minutes before carving, then cut it into portions and arrange it on a warm serving platter. Add the orange juice and vinegar (if using) to the roasting pan and mix with the cooking juices, and cooked apples and currants. Spoon this mixture over the chicken. Garnish with orange wedges, if desired.

CUNNING COOKS

Capulet: Sirrah, go hire me twenty cunning cooks.
Servant: You shall have none ill, sir, for I'll try if they can lick their fingers.
Capulet: How canst thou try them so?
Servant: Marry, sir, 'tis an ill cook that cannot lick his own fingers; therfore he that cannot lick his fingers goes not with me.

—Romeo and Juliet

Roast Chicken Stuffed with Veal and Pistachios

Either a deboned turkey breast or a large deboned roasting chicken is ideal to use in this recipe, which adds pistachios, artichoke bottoms, and pine nuts to the veal stuffing. If sweet chestnuts are in season, they make an attractive addition; if not, simply add a few more pistachios.

Other forcing for any dainty Fowl; as Turky, Chickens, or Phesants, or the like, boild or roste

from *The Accomplisht Cook* by Robert May

Take minced veal raw, and bacon or beef suet minced with it; being finely minced, season it with cloves and mace, a few corrans, salt and some boild bottoms of artichocks cut in form of dice small, and mingle amonst the forcing, with pine-apple-seeds, pistaches, chesnuts and some raw eggs, and fill your poultrey, &c.

BALD AS A CHICKEN

Syphilis, which can result in hair loss, was sometimes treated with steam baths. Since the fool's mistress is a prostitute, "scald" takes on a new meaning.

All Servants: Gramercies, good
Fool; how does your mistress?
Fool: She's e'en setting on the
water to scald such chickens
as you are.

—*Timon of Athens*

Apart from its brothels, London had a real "Scalding Alley," so named because it was used by the poulterers near the Stocks Market to clean the birds sold at their stalls.

Our Version

1 roasting chicken (about 4-½–5 pounds)
Salt, to taste
2 rashers bacon

STUFFING
1 pound ground veal
3 rashers bacon, finely chopped
½ teaspoon ground cloves
½ teaspoon ground mace
¼ cup currants
6 small cooked artichoke bottoms, diced (a 14-ounce can)
2 tablespoons pine nuts
¼ cup pistachios
6 chestnuts, roasted, peeled, and quartered (optional)
1 egg
Salt, to taste

Debone the chicken, starting with the back. Remove the thigh bones from the inside, but leave the drumsticks in place for a more interesting presentation. Cut off the wings. Preheat the oven to 400°F.

Put the ground veal in a large bowl and add the remaining stuffing ingredients. Working with your hands, mix the stuffing until the texture is even. Distribute the stuffing evenly in the bird and then sew it closed with kitchen string and a poultry needle or pin it closed, making sure that the cavity is properly covered with skin.

Place the bird sewn side down in a greased roasting pan. Sprinkle a little salt on the skin and place the rashers of bacon over the breast. Roast in the oven for 15 minutes, then reduce the heat to 325°F and continue roasting for 1 hour. Baste occasionally.

apon with Orange Sauce

This recipe is really for an orange sauce to be served with chicken, which can be either boiled or roasted. Rather than boil a prime piece of poultry, we suggest using an old stewing hen to make the stock, or using commercial stock, then roasting a capon or large chicken.

To boyle a Capon with Orenges or Lemmons

from *A Book of Cookrye* by A.W.

Take your Capon and boyle him tender and take a little of the broth when it is boyled and put it into a pipkin with Mace and Sugar a good deale, and pare three Orenges and pil them and put them in your pipkin, and boile them a little among your broth, and thicken it with wine and yolkes of egges, and Sugar a good deale, and salt but a little, and set your broth no more on the fire for quailing, and serve it without sippets.

Our Version

STOCK

1 stewing hen
1 onion, quartered
A few sprigs of parsley
4 peppercorns
4 allspice berries
1 teaspoon salt

THE MULTI-PURPOSE CAPON: BRIBE OR BROODER

Jaques: All the world's a stage,
...And then the justice,
In fair round belly with good
capon lined,
With eyes severe and beard of
formal cut,
Full of wise saws and modern
instances;
And so he plays his part.

—*As You Like It*

In addition to being highly prized table birds suitable for offering as a bribe to the local justice, as Jaques suggests above, capons had a role in the farmyard. Gervase Markham tells us that capons were used to look after broods of chickens, ducks, and other fowl. A capon's size allowed it not only to nest 30 young at a time but also to effectively defend them against kites and buzzards.

In order to make a capon bond with its charges, one was instructed to "beate and sting all his breast and neather parts, and then in the darke to seate the Chickens under him, whose warmth taking away his smart, hee will fall much in love with them."

Wash the hen and put it in a large soup pot with the onion, parsley, peppercorns, allspice, and salt. Cover with cold water. Bring to a boil and remove the scum. Simmer for about 1 hour on medium heat. Remove the hen and strain the stock.

SAUCE

- 4 cups stock
- 1 teaspoon ground mace
- 2 tablespoons sugar
- 2 oranges, peeled
- 1 lemon, peeled
- ¼ cup white wine
- 3 egg yolks
- ½ cup sugar
- Salt, to taste

Put the stock in a clean pot. Add mace, 2 tablespoons sugar, and peeled whole oranges and lemon. It's important to remove all of the white pith from the citrus fruits or the sauce will taste bitter. Bring to a boil and simmer for 15 to 20 minutes. Turn off the heat.

Whisk together white wine, egg yolks, ½ cup sugar, and salt. Add ½ cup of the warm broth and whisk. Then whisk the egg mixture into the pot of broth.

Serving suggestion: Cut up a roast chicken and arrange the pieces on a platter with sippets (small triangles of toast) around the edge. Pour a little sauce over the chicken pieces and garnish with orange slices. Serve remaining sauce in a gravy boat.

Pies, Tarts, and Pasties

Pastry Triumphs and Trophies

PIES DOMINATED the Elizabethan dining table, grand or lowly. Meats were baked in a crust to keep them moist. Fruits were often pre-baked in a crust to soften them before they were puréed and seasoned to fill a tart. Pies were the casserole dishes of the day, carried to the table and then opened with a flourish and their contents scooped out.

"Eating humble pie" wasn't just a figure of speech to Elizabethans. Almost every cookbook of the period offers instructions "to make a Pye of Humbles," or guts, particularly deer guts. One cook, John Murrell, even suggests: "for want of Umbles to doe it with a Lambes head and Purtenance [tail]." These pies would have been served to the less prestigious diners sitting on benches at the lowest table, while those at the head table ate more delicate pies made with choice cuts of meat.

Small pies or pasties could be made for individual servings, but for a truly grand presentation a cook would raise a large coffin, a free-standing crust made of boiled pastry that was draped over a form until it stiffened into shape.

These grand pies evolved into spectacular showpieces that not only fed the guests, but also provided the evening's entertainment. Robert May opens his authoritative cookbook with a chapter entitled "Triumphs and Trophies in Cookery, to be used at Festival Times, as Twelfth Day, &tc.," in which he describes a bizarre battle scene–cum–food fight rendered in pastry.

Combining the art of the pastry chef and pyrotechnic wizardry, this after-dinner entertainment requires the construction of three huge pastry sculptures. First there is the pastry-covered ship of war, complete with cannons that fire real gunpowder. Next is the hollow stag sculpted out of pastry "with a broad arrow in the side of him, and his body filled up with claret wine." Then comes the "Castle with Battlements, Percullices, Gates, and Draw Bridges," also outfitted with lines of gunpowder. Surrounding these are smaller pies filled with live birds and frogs, as well as hollowed eggshells filled with rosewater.

At the conclusion of the meal "some of the Ladies may be perswaded to pluck the Arrow out of the Stag, then will the Claret wine follow as blood running out of a wound. This being done with admiration to the beholders, after some short pawse, fire the train of the Castle, that the pieces all of one side may go off; then fire the trains of one side of the Ship as in a Battle."

After the battle, "to sweeten the stinck of the powder, the Ladies take the egg shells full of sweet waters and throw them at each other. All dangers being seemed over, by this time you may suppose they well desire to see what is in the pies; where lifting first the lid off one pie, out skips some Frogs, which makes the Ladies to skip and shreek; next after the other pie, when comes out the Birds; who by a natural instinct flying at the light, will put out the candles: so that what with the flying Birds and skipping Frogs, the one above, the other beneath, will cause much delight and pleasure to the whole company: at length the candles are lighted, and a Banquet [dessert] brought in, the musick sounds, and every one with much delight and content rehearses their actions in the former passages."

Although this pastry extravaganza sounds almost ludicrous in its excess, to May it embodied all that was grand and gracious during the reigns of Elizabeth I and the Stuarts, before England was torn apart by civil war in the 1640s and these playful theatrics were eclipsed by the austere morality of the Puritans. May wistfully concludes: "These were formerly the delights of the Nobility, before good House-keeping had left England, and the Sword really acted that which was onely counterfeited in such honest and laudable Exercises as these."

Hark, villains, I will grind your bones to dust,
And with your blood and it I'll make a paste,
And of the paste a coffin I will rear,
And make two pasties of your shameful heads,
And bid that strumpet, your unhallowed dam,
Like to the earth swallow her own increase.

—Titus Andronicus

On Making Pastry

...nothing can we call our own but death,
And that small model of the barren earth
Which serves as paste and cover to our Bones.
—Richard II

The following instructions for making boiled pastry crust—like that still used in traditional English pork pies—appear in a chapter on baked meats, with a selection of venison, veal, poultry, and other fillings.

This thick, tough dough was stiff enough to hold its shape when formed into tall, free-standing pies, often of massive dimensions. These pastry shells were known as coffins and were used to bake everything from eels to apples.

Modern cooks who shape their crusts in pie plates seldom use boiled crust, but we have provided this recipe for those who seek a truly authentic presentation. This crust works well with thick meat fillings such as in the Pig Pie (see page 130).

For most pies we recommend the Flaky Pastry made with minimal amounts of cold water.

Tart shells were often sculpted into ornamental shapes using a firm pastry such as the Sweet Pastry.

To make Paste, and to raise Coffins

from *The Good Huswifes Handmaide for the Kitchin* attributed to John Partridge

Take fine flower, and lay it on a boord, and take a certaine of yolkes of Egges as your quantitie of flower is, then take a certaine of Butter and water, and boil them together, but ye must take heed ye put not too many yolks of Egges, for if you doe, it will make it drie and not pleasant in eating: and yee must take heed ye put not in too much Butter for if you doe, it will make it so fine and short that you cannot raise. And this paste is good to raise all maner of Coffins: Likewise if ye bake Venison, bake it in the past above named.

Our Version

BOILED CRUST

1-½ cups all-purpose flour	½ cup water
1 teaspoon salt	¼ cup lard
1 egg	¼ cup butter

Prepare your pie crusts the day before you need them. First make the shapes by covering a jar or large tin (such as an apple juice can) with a piece of parchment paper. Then prepare the pastry. Sift the flour and salt together in a large bowl. Make a well in the mixture and break the egg into the well, then bury it in the flour.

In a small saucepan boil the water, lard, and butter together. Pour the boiling mixture into the flour and egg. Stir with a fork or knife until completely blended. Reserve about one-quarter of the dough for the lid, wrap it in plastic, and set it aside. Roll out the remaining dough no thinner than ½ inch and drape it over the paper-covered jar or tin. Put it in a cool place, leaving it uncovered to dry and harden for at least 8 hours.

When you are ready to bake the pie, invert the crust onto a baking sheet and add the filling. Roll out the top crust. Wet the edges and crimp. Cut a vent hole and bake.

BRIDAL PIE

The origins of the multi-tiered wedding cake can be glimpsed in May's recipe for a multi-tiered "Bride Pie, of severall Compounds, being several distinct pies on one bottom." This behemoth party pie was constructed of an assortment of fillings. Some sections are filled with cockscombs, sweetbreads, and lamb kidneys, others with prawns, cockles, and pickled mushrooms. Another contains small stuffed birds. Another serves up artichoke bottoms. One of the pies contains the party trick: The cook is instructed to remove the bottom of this hollow pie "and put in live birds, or a snake, which will seem strange to the beholders, which cut up the Pie at the table. This is onely for a Wedding to pass away time." Frogs and bats were also popular in these prank pies that date back to the Middle Ages and were described in the popular nursery rhyme "Four and Twenty Black Birds."

FLAKY PASTRY

1-½ cups all-purpose flour
Pinch of salt
½ cup cold butter
¼ cup shortening
1 egg yolk
2 tablespoons ice water

Sift the flour and salt into a large bowl, then gently work in the butter and shortening until the mixture has reached the texture of coarse sand. Mix the egg yolk with 2 tablespoons of ice water. Pour the egg mixture into the flour mixture, then mix until the dough forms a ball. Do not overwork the dough. Crumbly dough makes for a flakier crust. It may be necessary to sprinkle in a little more cold water, but try not to let the dough become too wet or it will become hard when cooked. Let the dough rest, chilled, for 30 minutes before using.

SWEET PASTRY

½ cup sugar
½ cup butter
1 teaspoon vanilla
2 eggs
½ teaspoon salt
1 teaspoon baking powder
2-½ cups flour

Cream the sugar and butter. Beat in the vanilla and eggs. Mix the salt and baking powder with the flour and add it to the butter mixture, working until fully blended. This dough rolls out easily to fill all sorts of tart pans and is excellent with fruit filling.

This recipe makes enough pastry for two 9-inch tart shells. Bake them blind (empty) in an oven set at 350°F before adding the filling.

lmond Tart

The devil speed him! no man's pie is freed
From his ambitious finger
—HENRY VIII

We adapted Robert May's recipe by using beaten egg whites to make this sweet tart seem lighter. A little raspberry jam or preserves is another addition in keeping with the period.

To make an Almond Tart

from *The Accomplisht Cook* by Robert May

Strain beaten almonds with cream, yolks of eggs, sugar, cinamon, and ginger, boil it thick and fill your tart.

Our Version

Flaky pastry for a 9-inch pie
(see recipe page 124)
4 eggs
1 cup ground almonds
⅔ cup sugar
1 teaspoon cinnamon
½ teaspoon ginger
3 tablespoons raspberry jam (optional)

Preheat oven to 350°F. Roll out pastry, line tart pan, and prick the pastry with a fork. Separate the eggs. Mix the almonds, egg yolks, sugar, cinnamon, and ginger. Beat the egg whites until they form stiff peaks, then fold the egg whites into the almond mixture. Spread the jam on the pastry (if using), then pour the egg and almond mixture into the pastry and bake until set and golden, about 40 minutes.

FRENZY

The poet's eye, in a fine frenzy rolling,
Doth glance from heaven to earth, from earth to heaven;
And as imagination bodies forth
The form of things unknown, the poet's pen
Turns them to shapes, and gives to aery nothing
A local habitation and a name.

—A Midsummer Night's Dream

Friday Pie

Orlando: Then love me, Rosalind.
Rosalind: Yes, faith, will I, Fridays and Saturdays and all.
—As You Like It

Beets replace meat in this pie for fasting days. "Green Beetes" probably means "young" beets, rather than describing their colour. We chose to add orange juice to the pie filling before cooking to help plump up the raisins. More can be added at the end.

A Fridays Pye, without eyther Flesh or Fish

from *A New Booke of Cookerie* by John Murrell

Wash green Beetes cleane, picke out the middle string, and chop them small with two or three well relisht ripe Apples. Season it with Pepper, Salt, and Ginger: then take a good handfull of Razins of the Sunne, and put all in a Coffin of fine Paste, with a piece of sweet Butter, and so bake it: but before you serve it in, cut it up, and wring in the juyce of an Orenge and Sugar.

Our Version

- 3 medium beets
- Dash of white vinegar
- Flaky pastry for a covered 9-inch pie (see recipe page 124) or commercially prepared pie crust
- 3–6 apples, depending on size
- ½ cup raisins
- 1 teaspoon ginger
- 1 teaspoon salt
- ½ teaspoon pepper
- ½ cup sugar
- 1 orange, for 1 teaspoon zest, plus juice
- 1 teaspoon arrowroot flour or cornstarch
- 3 tablespoons butter

Wash the beets, but do not peel. Place them in a small saucepan covered with cold water and a dash of white vinegar. Boil the beets for roughly 25 minutes, then rinse under cool water.

Roll out the pastry and line the pie plate. Preheat oven to 325°F.

Finely dice the cooled beets into raisin-sized pieces. Peel, core, and slice the apples, then add them to the beets. Mix in raisins, ginger, salt, pepper, sugar, orange zest, and orange juice. Stir in the arrowroot flour or cornstarch.

Place the filling in the pie shell. Dab the butter on top of the filling, then cover it with the top crust. Bake for about 1 hour.

FRENZY REMEDY

We hope that this imaginative, though somewhat painful, treatment from Gervase Markham's *The English Housewife* was not inflicted on too many passionate poets: "For frenzie or inflammation of the calles of the braine you shal cause the juice of Beets to be with a serriudge squitted up into the patients nostrels, which wil purge and cleanse his head exceedingly; and give them to drinke posset ale, in which violet leave and lettice hath beene boiled, and it will sodainely bring him to a verie temperate mildnesse, and make the passion of frenzie forsake him."

Spinach Tortellini

Shakespeare may have developed a taste for Italian food at the Oliphant, an Italian inn in south London, according to biographer Anthony Holden. Elizabethan epicures were certainly familiar with pasta and Robert May gives four different recipes for tortellini stuffed with various combinations, including minced capon and calf's udder, pork and parsnip, and peas or beans. Our favourite, however, is this spinach version.

PLATT'S PASTA

The consummate entrepreneur Hugh Platt boasts of selling a new food product to Sir Francis Drake for use on a recent voyage. He describes a "certaine victuall in the forme of hollow pipes, or wafers" that is "very durable," "exceeding light," "cheape," and fully boiled in 30 minutes, ready to dress with oil or butter. In all probability this is pasta.

PINCHED PASTY

I will confess what I know without constraint. If ye pinch me like a pasty, I can say no more.

—All's Well That Ends Well

Tortelleti, or little Pasties

from *The Accomplisht Cook* by Robert May

Being washed and wrung dry, fry them in butter, put to them some sweet herbs chopped small with some grated parmisan, some cinamon, cloves, saffron, pepper, currans, raw eggs, and grated bread: Make your pasties, and boil them in strong broth, cream, milk or almond milk: thus you may do any fish. Serve them with sugar, cinamon and grated cheese.

Our Version

FILLING

8 ounces spinach
⅓ cup Parmesan cheese
Pinch each of cinnamon, ground cloves, and pepper
Pinch of saffron (optional)
1 tablespoon currants (optional)
1 egg
2–3 tablespoons bread crumbs

Pasta Dough	
1-½ cups semolina flour for pasta	¼ cup water (or 1 egg white if making dough by hand)
½ teaspoon salt	1 tablespoon olive oil
1 egg	

Egg Wash	
1 egg	Water

To prepare the filling, wash and pick the spinach, then cook it in a large covered pan with very little water until it is completely wilted. Drain well. Chop it finely and then add the seasonings, egg, and just enough bread crumbs to soak up any moisture.

Because of the lengthy kneading time—10 minutes—we recommend making the pasta dough in a bread maker. Follow the instructions on your bread maker and remove the dough after kneading.

Divide the dough into 2 or 3 portions and wrap them in plastic wrap. It dries out quickly, so only work with one portion at a time. Using a heavy rolling pin, roll the dough out, rolling away from you and frequently lifting and turning the sheet of dough so that it rolls out evenly. It should be nearly paper-thin. Using the rim of a drinking glass, cut circles out of the dough. Beat the remaining egg with a little water and brush the egg wash halfway around the edge of each pasta circle. Spoon a little of the spinach filling into the centre of the circle, being careful not to overfill. Fold the pasta into a half moon and press the edges together. Makes about 60 tortellini.

To cook the tortellini, bring 6–8 cups of chicken stock or salted water to a boil in a large pan. Cook the tortellini, one layer at a time, for about 10 to 12 minutes, or until tender.

MAKING DOUGH BY HAND

If you don't have a bread maker, you can make the dough by hand. Substitute an egg white for the ¼ cup water. Put the flour in a large mixing bowl with the salt. Make a well in the centre and put in the egg, egg white, and oil, then mix it together with your fingers until it forms a ball. Sprinkle a few drops of cold water on any dry bits and work them into the ball. Knead the dough for 10 minutes on a floured board. Incorporate more flour if the dough feels sticky. Eventually the dough should be elastic but not sticky, so that you can roll it out with minimal flour.

Pig Pie

Starting with ground pork from the supermarket takes most of the work out of this recipe, but for a leaner pie we suggest starting with a whole piece of meat and then trimming and grinding it yourself.

To make a Pig pye

from *The Accomplisht Ladys Delight* by Hannah Woolley

Flea your Pig, and cut it into pieces, and season it with Pepper, Salt, Nutmeg and large Mace, lay into your Coffin good store of Raisins of the Sun, and Currans, and fill it up with sweet butter, so close it, and serve it hot.

LONG-LIVED PIES

Large feasts could go on for days and dishes left over from one meal often made return appearances on menus in the following days. One cookbook gives instructions "to make a pie to keep long" by placing parboiled, seasoned meat in a very thick pastry made of rye flour, with a small hole left in the top crust. After baking the pie for 2 hours, the cook is instructed to pour in as much vinegar as the pie can hold, then stop up the hole with more pastry and return the pie to the oven for another 2 hours.

cont'd on p. 131

Our Version

Flaky pastry for a covered 9-inch pie (see recipe page 124) or boiled crust (see recipe page 123)
1-½ pounds pork (leg or butt is suitable)
½ cup raisins
¼ cup currants
1 teaspoon grated nutmeg
½ teaspoon grated mace
Salt and pepper, to taste
Butter

Roll out the pastry and line the pie plate. Preheat the oven to 325°F.

Trim off excess fat and chop the pork, or grind it roughly in a food processor. Wash raisins and currants, then add them to the raw meat with the seasonings. Place the meat mixture in the pie shell. Dot a little butter on top of the filling. The leaner the meat, the more butter will be needed to keep it tender. Put on the top crust. Bake for 1 hour.

Hamlet refers to this practice when he comments that the left-over food from his father's funeral reappears at the feast to celebrate his mother's remarriage.

Horatio: My lord, I came to see your father's funeral.
Hamlet: I prithee do not mock me, fellow student.
I think it was to see my mother's wedding.
Horatio: Indeed, my lord, it followed hard upon.
Hamlet: Thrift, thrift, Horatio. The funeral bak't meats
Did coldly furnish forth the marriage tables.
Would I had met my dearest foe in heaven
Or ever I had seen that day, Horatio!

THE GREAT PUMPKIN

Costard the clown, acting the role of Pompey in a play within a play, describes himself as a great gourd in this malapropism from *Love's Labour's Lost:* "O Lord, sir, the parties themselves, the actors, sir, will show whereuntil it doth amount. For mine own part, I am, as they say, but to parfect one man in one poor man, Pompion the Great, sir."

Pumpkin Pie

His mother was a vot'ress of my order,
And in the spiced Indian air, by night,
Full often hath she gossip'd by my side,
And sat with me on Neptune's yellow sands,
Marking th'embarked traders on the flood;
—A Midsummer Night's Dream

This recipe is remarkably similar to the pumpkin pie that we eat today, with the pumpkin flesh first cooked until soft, then baked in a custard-like filling with spices.

To make Tart of Pompeons

from *Epulario* by Giovanne de Rosselli

Take Pompeons and make them cleane and grate them as you doe Cheese, and boile them a little in broth or in milk, then take as much new Cheese as aforesaid, adde to it also a little old Cheese, take also a pound of the panch of a Hogge, or a Cowes Udder well sodden and chopped small, and if you will you may use Butter instead of those two thinges aforesaid, or Suet, adding unto it halfe a pound of Sugar, a little Saffron and Sinamon with a quart of milk, and Egges, as need requireth. And when you thinke the Pompeons are sodden take them up and straine them, and colour it with a little Saffron, then making a crust of paste under it, put it in a pan, and make a soft fire both under and over it, and being halfe baked, cover it with Wafers or such like stuffe in stead of an upper crust, and being thorow baked, straw it with Sugar and Rosewater.

Our Version

Flaky pastry for a 9-inch pie
(see recipe page 124),
or commercial pie dough
2 eggs
¾ cup extra-fine ricotta cheese
1-½ cups canned plain pumpkin
1 cup brown sugar
Pinch of saffron
1-½ teaspoons cinnamon
½ teaspoon ginger (optional)

Preheat the oven to 350°F. Roll out the pastry and line a 9-inch pie plate. Beat the eggs, then stir in the ricotta and pumpkin until completely blended. Stir in the brown sugar, saffron, cinnamon, and ginger (if using), and pour into the pie shell. Bake in the oven until the filling is set, about 60 to 70 minutes.

For a deep-dish pie increase the pumpkin to 2 cups, increase the ricotta to 1 cup, and add another egg. If you prefer a creamier filling, substitute ¼ cup 35% cream for ¼ cup of the ricotta or substitute mascarpone for the ricotta.

DECORATIVE PUMPKINS AND OTHER FRUITS

In 1581 Queen Elizabeth I had a special banquet house erected on the grounds of Westminster. The canvas ceiling was painted to depict a sky full of clouds, stars, and sunbeams. From it hung wicker vines bearing gilded flowers, pomegranates, oranges, pumpkins, and cucumbers.

Turkey Pie

Excellent picnic fare, this pie is well spiced to be flavourful when eaten cold. Rather than stuffing and baking a whole deboned bird, we suggest making this pie in two layers: a boneless turkey breast on the bottom, covered with a layer of minced veal.

To bake Turkey, Chicken, Pea-Chicken, Pheasant Pouts, Heath Pouts, Caponets, or Partridge for to be eaten cold

from *The Accomplisht Cook* by Robert May

Take a turkey chicken, bone it and lard it with pretty big lard, a pound and half will serve, then season it with an ounce of pepper, an ounce of nutmegs, and two ounces of salt, lay some butter in the bottom of the pie, then lay on the fowl and put in it six or eight whole cloves, then put on all the seasoning with good store of butter, close it up, and baste it over with eggs, bake it, and being baked fill it up with clarified butter.

Thus you may bake them for to be eaten hot, giving them but half the seasoning, and liquor it with gravy and juyce of orange.

Bake this pie in fine paste; for more variety you may make a stuffing for it as followeth; mince some beef-suet and a little veal very fine, some sweet herbs, grated nutmeg, pepper, salt, two or three raw yolks of eggs, some boild skirrets or pieces of artichocks, grapes or gooseberries, &tc.

DRESSED FOR DINNER

In 1586 the Earl of Leicester, acting as the governor general of the queen's forces in the low countries, hosted a dinner to mark the feast of Saint George. Although Elizabeth I was not in attendance, a place was set in her honour. Holinshed records the rest: "The side tables being furnished all in silver plate, and attended on by gentlemen, sundrie sorts of musikes continued the interim of the first course, which doone and avoided, the trumpets sounded in for the second, which was all baked meats of beasts, and foules; the beasts as lions, dragons, leopards, and such like, bearing the veins of arms, and the foules, as pecocks, swans, phesants, turkie cocks and others in their naturall fethers, spred as in their greatest pride, which sight was rare and magnificent."

Our Version

Flaky pastry for a covered 10-inch pie (see recipe page 124)	1 egg
	Milk

For Turkey Layer

1 turkey breast (approximately 2 pounds)	¼ teaspoon ground nutmeg
¼ teaspoon pepper	¼ teaspoon ground cloves
¼ teaspoon salt	2 tablespoons butter

For Veal Layer

1 pound ground veal	Salt and pepper, to taste
⅓ cup finely chopped parsley	2 medium cooked parsnips, diced (about ½ cup)
2 tablespoons chopped chives or green onion	⅓ cup grapes
Pinch of nutmeg	3 rashers streaky bacon, diced

Roll out pastry and line the pie dish. Debone the turkey breast and remove the skin. Don't worry if the meat doesn't stay in one piece, as it may need to be trimmed to fit in an even layer in the pie. Combine the pepper, salt, nutmeg, and cloves, then sprinkle them on the turkey. Arrange the turkey in the bottom of the pie in as even a layer as possible, then dot with butter.

Preheat the oven to 375°F. Mix the veal with the parsley, chives or green onion, nutmeg, salt and pepper, parsnips, grapes, and bacon. Arrange the veal mixture on top of the turkey. Cover with pastry. Crimp the edges, cut a vent, and brush with egg beaten with milk.

Bake for 20 minutes. Reduce the heat to 350°F and bake for 1 hour. If the pastry begins to brown at the edges before the pie is done, cover the top with foil.

O, Peace! Contemplation makes a rare turkey-cock of him. How he jets under his advanc'd plumes!

—*Twelfth Night*

From the Dairy

Almond Cheesecake

Trust none;
For oaths are straws, men's faiths are wafer-cakes
—Henry V

In addition to the simple almond cheesecake described here, Robert May also tells readers how to make variations with "Holland cheese" (Edam), currants, pistachios, and elderflowers.

IN THE HEAT OF THE OVEN

An oven that is stopp'd, or river stayed,
Burneth more hotly, swelleth with more rage

—*Venus and Adonis*

To make Cheesecakes

from *The Accomplisht Cook* by Robert May

Let your paste be very good, either puff-paste or cold butter paste, with sugar mixed with it; then the whey being dryed very well from the cheese curds which must be made of new milk or better, beat them in a mortar or tray, with a quarter of a pound of butter to every pottle of curds, a good quantity of rose water, three grains of ambergreece or musk prepared, the crumbs of a small manchet rubbed through a cullender, the yoks of ten eggs, a grated nutmeg, a little salt, a good store of sugar, mix all these well together with a little cream, but do not make them too soft; instead of bread you may take almonds which are much better; bake them in a quick oven, and let them not stand too long in lest they should be too dry.

Our Version

Flaky pastry to line the bottom of a springform pan (see recipe page 124)
1 pound pressed cottage cheese
4 egg yolks
⅓ cup cream
1 egg
½ cup sugar
1 teaspoon almond essence
1 teaspoon grated nutmeg
½ teaspoon salt
½ cup ground almonds
½ cup sliced almonds

Preheat the oven to 350°F. Line the bottom of a springform pan with pastry, prick it all over with a fork, and bake for 15 minutes, or until golden.

While the pastry is baking mix the cottage cheese with the egg yolks, cream, egg, and sugar. Stir in the almond essence, nutmeg, salt, and ground almonds. When the pastry is ready, pour the cheese mixture over it. Return it to the oven and reduce the temperature to 325°F. Bake for 30 minutes, then top with the sliced almonds. Return to the oven and cook until the filling is set, about 30 minutes longer.

Cheese Puffs

Why my cheese, my digestion, why hast thou not serv'd thyself in to my table so many meals?
—Troilus and Cressida

This simple recipe produces small cheesecake-like morsels that make a great appetizer or snack, although Elizabethans believed that serving cheese at the end of meal aided digestion.

To make Puffes on the English Fashion

from *A New Booke of Cookerie* by John Murrell

Take new Milke curds, presse out the Whay cleane, take the yolkes of three Egges, and the white of one, fine Wheat-floure, and mingle amongst your Curdes. Season it with Nutmeg, Sugar, and Rosewater, mingle all together. Butter a fayre white Paper, lay a spoonefull at once upon it, set them into a warme Oven, not over hot, when you see them rise as high as a halfepeny loafe, then take Rosewater, and Butter, and indale them over: scrape on Sugar, and set them in the Oven againe, until they be dryed at the tops like yce. Then take them out, and serve them upon a Plate, either at Dinner or Supper.

CANDLELIGHT DINING

Tapers they are, with your sweet breath puff'd out.

—Love's Labour's Lost

Hugh Platt gives us this tip on preventing the unpleasant smell of tallow from ruining your next dinner party. Dip cheap tallow candles in a coat of beeswax. If making candles at home, adding turmeric to the tallow will give your candles that expensive beeswax hue.

For a more elaborate presentation sure to thrill your guests, take a long piece of wire and, starting at the bottom of the candle, thread it through the middle of the wick and out the top. Wrap the excess wire around the wooden beams of your dining room ceiling. The candles, when lit, will seem to float in the air.

Platt does not, however, offer any tips on preventing the hot wax from dripping on the food or on your guests' heads.

Our Version

¾ cup ricotta cheese
3 egg yolks
1 egg white
⅓ cup all-purpose flour
1 teaspoon nutmeg

TOPPING
1 tablespoon rosewater or liqueur (such as amaretto)
¼ cup sugar

Mix first five ingredients until smooth. Drop spoonfuls of batter onto a prepared cookie sheet, preferably lined with silicone paper. Bake in the oven at 350°F for 15 to 20 minutes. When the puffs have risen, brush them with rosewater or liqueur, sprinkle with sugar, then return to oven until golden.

Cinnamon Pudding

Speed: Item, She hath no teeth.
Launce: I care not for that neither, because I love crusts.
—Two Gentlemen of Verona

This creamy bread pudding flavoured with cinnamon would have been served towards the end of a meal, but without the crusts and soft enough for Launce's lady.

OF SPICE AND SIN

Clown: Then fare thee well, I must go buy spices for our sheep-shearing.
Autolycus: Prosper you, sweet sir! Your purse is not hot enough to purchase your spice.

—The Winter's Tale

The clown doesn't realize it, but he has just had his money stolen by a professional con artist. Shakespeare apparently modelled the techniques that Autolycus employs on those described in pamphlets about the lives of rogues and "coney-catchers."

Another Pudding, called Cinamon Pudding

from *The Accomplisht Cook* by Robert May

Take five penny loaves, and searce them through a cullender, put them in a deep dish or tray, and put to them five pints of cream, cinamon six ounces, suet one pound minced, eggs six yolks, four whites, sugar, salt, slict dates, stamped almonds, or none, rose-water.

Our Version

½ loaf white bread, torn into ½-inch pieces
2–3 tablespoons cinnamon
10 sliced dates
2 cups 10% cream
1 egg
½ cup sugar
½ teaspoon salt
¼ cup ground almonds

Preheat the oven to 325°F. Trim the crust from the bread and tear it into crumbs; you should have about 6 cups of crumbs. Put the crumbs in a casserole dish. Sprinkle the cinnamon on the crumbs and add the dates. Toss until well mixed.

Blend the cream, egg, sugar, and salt. Pour over the bread. Sprinkle with ground almonds. Bake for 30 minutes.

Baked Custard Tart with Raisins

Parolles: I know not how I have deserve'd to run into my lord's displeasure.
Lafew: You have made shift to run into't, boots and spurs and all, like him that leapt into the custard...
—All's Well That Ends Well

Custard has been a source of slapstick comedy from Shakespeare to the Three Stooges. This rich and velvety-smooth custard was probably served in a pie crust, but it is equally good when baked in individual ramekins.

SPECIAL EFFECTS

Elizabethans knew how to have a rip-roaring good time, and Shakespeare had some stiff competition for public entertainment. Celebrations often started with a parade followed by jousting and archery contests. Drums, guns, and fireworks were often added to the mix along with dancing and music.

In the following passage we glimpse but part of an elaborate pageant staged for the queen that pitched the Forces of Beauty against the Forces of Desire. The cannons belonging to Desire "were shot off, the one with sweet powder, and the other with sweet water, verie odoriferous and pleasant, and

cont'd on p. 145

How to bake Custards

from *A Book of Cookrye* by A.W.

Take to every pinte of Cream five Egs, and put in no whites, and straine your Cream and Egges together, season it with Cloves & mace and sugar, and when your paste is well hardened in the Oven, having small raisins & dates put in your stuffe, and let it not bake too much, for much baking will make your Custard to quaile, or els to fall. Doucets after the same sort.

Our Version

Flaky pastry for 9-inch pie plate (see recipe page 124), or commercially prepared crust
2 cups 18% cream
4 whole cloves
2 pieces whole mace
5 egg yolks
⅓ cup sugar
½ cup raisins

Preheat the oven to 350°F. Bake the crust blind (or empty). To ensure that the pastry keeps its shape, prick it all over with a fork. Cut a circle of paper to fit inside the bottom of the pie plate. Place the circle over the pastry and cover it with dried beans or pastry weights. Bake until the pastry is light brown (about 20 minutes), then remove from the oven. Reduce the heat to 225°F.

While the pastry is baking prepare the custard. Warm the cream in a saucepan with the cloves and mace for about 15 minutes. Do not boil. Whisk the egg yolks with the sugar. Remove the cream from the heat. Ladle a small amount of warm cream into the egg yolks and stir well. Then pour the egg yolk mixture into the saucepan of warm cream. Return to the stove over low heat, stirring until slightly thickened.

Sprinkle the raisins in the bottom of the pastry crust, or earthenware ramekins, then pour in the custard. Bake until the custard is set, about 30 minutes.

the noise of the shooting was verie excellent consent of melodie within the mount. And after that was a store of prettie scaling ladders, and the footmen threw floures and such fancies against the wals, with all such devices as might seeme fit shot for desire."

For summer festivals and special occasions whole streets came alive with a party atmosphere, as we can see from Machin's description of the proclamation of Queen Elizabeth I: "at after-non, all the chyrches in London dyd ryng, and at nyght dyd make bonefyres and set tabulls in the street, and ded att and drink and mad mere for the newe quen Elsabeth."

Cheese Tart

A dried-out piece of cheese can be put to good use in this recipe, which instructs cooks to pare the cheese in slices and soak it in milk to soften it.

Elizabethans typically served sweet and savoury pies in the same course. This recipe calls for sugar, but a savoury variation could also be made by substituting herbs. Similar cheese tart recipes call for the addition of flowers such as parboiled borage blossoms or marigolds.

STARVED JUSTICE

Several scholars have suggested that Shallow, the comic country justice described here by Falstaff, came out of Shakespeare's real-life encounters with the law.

Falstaff: I do remember him at Clement's Inn, like a man made after supper of a cheese-paring. When 'a was naked, he was for all the world like a fork'd redish, with a head fantastically carv'd upon it with a knife.

—2 Henry IV

To make a Tart of Cheese

from *A Proper New Booke of Cookery*

Take harde Chese and cut it in slices, and pare it, then lay it in fayre water, or in sweete mylke, the space of three houres, then take it up, and break it in a morter till it be small, then draw it up through a strayner, with the yolkes of six egges, and season it up with Suger and sweet butter, and so bake it.

Our Version

Flaky pastry for 9-inch pie (see recipe page 124), or a commercial pie crust

FOR SWEET VERSION

2-¼ cups grated cheddar cheese
½ teaspoon nutmeg
3 tablespoons sugar
¼ cup raisins (optional)
1 egg
2 egg yolks
1 cup milk or light cream

FOR SAVOURY VERSION

2-¼ cups grated cheddar cheese, preferably old
½ teaspoon salt
¼ cup finely chopped fresh parsley and chives
1 egg
2 egg yolks
1 cup milk or light cream

Preheat the oven to 325°F. Roll out the pastry and line a 9-inch pie plate. If you are making the sweet version, toss the grated cheese with the nutmeg, sugar, and raisins (if using). If you are making the savoury version, toss the grated cheese with the salt, parsley, and chives. Put the cheese mixture in the unbaked pastry shell.

Beat the egg and yolks with the cream and pour over the cheese mixture. Bake for 35 minutes.

TIME TO EAT

...the sixt hour, when beasts most graze, birds best peck, and men sit down to that nourishment which is called supper...

—*Love's Labour's Lost*

"An houre is suffycyent to syt at dynner; and not so long at supper," says Andrew Boorde. "Englande hath an evyll use in syttunge longe at dyner and at supper." Despite this caution the business lunch was already well established among Londoners, who were known to sit until 2 or 3 in the afternoon.

Norfolk Fool

...thou full dish of fool...
—Troilus and Cressida

This rich and creamy dessert resembles an unbaked bread pudding spiced with cinnamon.

A Norfolk Fool

from *The English Housewife* by Gervase Markham

Take a pint of the sweetest and thickest Creame that can be gotten, and set it on the fire in a very clean scowred skillet, and put into it suger, cinamon, and a nutmeg cut into four quarters, and so boyle it well: then take the yolkes of foure eggs, and take off the filmes, and beate them well with a little sweete creame: then take the foure quarters of the nutmeg out of the creame, then put in the egges, and stirre it exceedingly, till it be thicke: then take a fine Manchet, and cut it into thin shives, as much as will cover a dish-bottome, and, holding it in your hand, powre halfe the creame into the dish: then lay your bread over it, then cover the bread with the rest of the creame, and so let it stand till it be cold: then strow it over with caraway Comfets, and prick up some cinnamon Comfets, and some slic't dates; or for want thereof, scrape all over it some suger, and trim the sides of the dish with suger and so serve it up.

Our Version

6 slices challah or good-quality white bread, trimmed of crust

CUSTARD

2-¼ cups 10% cream

½ cup sugar

2 cinnamon sticks

1 whole nutmeg, cut in quarters

4 egg yolks

TOPPING

1 tablespoon sugar

½ teaspoon ground cinnamon

5 dates (optional)

To make the custard, warm 2 cups of the cream in a saucepan with the sugar, cinnamon sticks, and nutmeg for about 10 minutes. Stir often and do not boil. Whisk the remaining cream with the egg yolks. Remove the nutmeg quarters and cinnamon sticks from the cream. Return the pan to low heat and whisk in the egg yolks. Take care not to leave it on the heat for too long. The custard will thicken only slightly, and should still be smooth and easy to pour.

Pour a little custard in the bottom of a 1-½-quart dish. Arrange some bread slices on top, then continue alternating bread and custard layers, ending with a layer of custard.

Mix the sugar and cinnamon and sprinkle it on top. Slice the dates and arrange them on top of the custard (if using). Chill until ready to serve.

Serving suggestion: Good with fresh fruit such as strawberries.

range Rice

Beatrice: The Count is neither sad, nor sick, nor merry, nor well; but civil count, civil as an orange, and something of that jealous complexion.
—MUCH ADO ABOUT NOTHING

Shakespeare intended "civil" as a homophone with Seville, the Spanish city where most of England's oranges originated. Yellow—not green—was the colour of jealousy to Elizabethans.

Oranges lend a refreshing quality to this sweet rice dish. Although the Elizabethan recipe title refers to a tart, the recipe describes a stuffing or filling that tastes best without a crust.

ANYTHING FOR AN ORANGE

The fact that orange trees were native to Mediterranean climates was no deterrent to the English gardeners who went to extraordinary lengths to keep them at home.

As Parkinson writes, "some keep them in great square boxes, and lift them to and fro by iron hooks on the sides, or cause them to be rowled by trundles, or small wheels under them, to place them in an house, or closed gallerie for the winter time: others plant them against a bricke wall in the ground, and defend them by a shed of boardes, covered over with feare-cloth in the winter, and by the warmth of a stove, or other such thing, give them some comfort in colder times: but no tent or meane provision will preserve them."

To make a Tart of Ryce

from *The Good Huswifes Jewell* by Thomas Dawson

Boyle your Rice, and put in the yokes of two or three Egges into the Rice, and when it is boyled, put it into a dish, and season it with Suger, Sinamon and Ginger, and butter, and the juyce of two or three Orenges, and set it on the fire againe.

Our Version

1 cup arborio rice
3 cups water
2 large juice oranges
½ cup sugar
3 egg yolks
½ teaspoon ground ginger
1 teaspoon ground cinnamon
2 tablespoons butter
½ teaspoon orange zest

Boil the rice in the water for 5 minutes, then turn down the heat to a low simmer and cover the pot. Simmer for 10 minutes, or until rice is tender.

In the meantime squeeze the juice from the oranges. Whisk the juice with the sugar, egg yolks, ginger, and cinnamon. Stir the butter into the pot with the rice, then stir in the egg and orange juice mixture and the orange zest. Return the pot to the stove-top and cook, stirring well, for 2 or 3 minutes until the sauce thickens slightly. Serve hot or cold, garnished with fresh orange slices, candied orange peel (see the recipe for Orange Comfits on page 204), or a little more orange zest.

Rice Pudding

By using rice flour instead of grains of rice, this pudding has a somewhat mealy texture similar to cream of wheat. It would have been easily gummed by the toothless.

COMFORT FOOD

**Adversity's sweet milk, philosophy,
To comfort thee though thou art
banished.**

—Romeo and Juliet

To make a Rice Pudding

from *The Accomplisht Ladys Delight* by Hannah Woolley

Take thin Cream, or good Milk, of what quantity you please, boyl it with a little Cinamon in it, and when it hath boyled a while, take out the Cinamon, and put in Rose-water, and Sugar enough to make it sweet and good; then having your Rice ready beaten as fine as Flower and Searced as some do it, strew it in, till it be the thickness of a Hasty Pudding, then pour it into a Dish, and serve it.

Our Version

1–2 cinnamon sticks
2 cups whole milk (or substitute cream for some or all of the milk)
¼ teaspoon rosewater
⅓ cup sugar
⅔ cup rice flour

Simmer cinnamon sticks in milk very gently for about 15 to 20 minutes. Do not boil or a skin will form on the milk. Stir in rosewater and sugar. Whisk in rice flour, adding about 1 tablespoon at a time until desired consistency is reached.

Roast Butter

Prince: Didst thou never see Titan kiss a dish of butter, pitiful-hearted Titan, that melted at the sweet tale of the sun's? If thou didst, then behold that compound.
—1 HENRY IV

Gervase Markham's bizzare-sounding recipe actually produces something that resembles a modern butter cookie. We found it much easier to make smaller cookie-shaped pieces than to attempt one large mass.

ALL ABOUT BUTTER

The best butter was a naturally yellow spring butter. To achieve this effect second-rate butter was coloured with marigolds and carrot juice. In *Delightes for Ladies,* Hugh Platt tells us we might make flavoured butters by mixing them with "a fewe drops of the extracted oile of Sage, Cinamon, Nutmegs, Mace, &c." Ever the salesman, he closes by saying we can find the instructions for making these oils in his other book, *The Jewel House of Art and Nature.*

To roast a pound of butter well

from *The English Housewife* by Gervase Markham

To roast a pound of Butter curiously and well, you shall take a pound of sweet Butter and beat it stiffe with sugar, and the yolkes of egges; then clap it round-wise about a spit, and lay it before a soft fire, and presently dredge it with the dredging before appointed for the Pigge [fine bread crumbs, currants, sugar, and salt mixed together]; then as it warmeth or melteth, so apply it with dredging till the Butter be overcomed and no more wil melt to fall from it, then roast it browne, and so draw it, and serve it out, the dish being as neatly trim'd with sugar as may be.

Our Version

½ cup butter	½ cup currants
½ cup sugar	1-½ cups bread crumbs
3 egg yolks	¼ teaspoon salt

FOR DREDGING

2 cups bread crumbs	½ teaspoon salt
½ cup sugar	

Preheat the oven to 300°F. Beat the butter and sugar together. When the mixture is creamy, beat in the egg yolks and then mix in the currants, bread crumbs, and salt. Mix the dredging ingredients on a plate. Shape the butter mixture into small balls about the size of loonies, then roll them in the dredging. Bake and watch closely. As the butter begins to melt and saturate the crumb coating, you will need to remove the cookies and roll them in the dredging again. They will flatten as they bake. Bake until golden and crunchy, about 40 minutes.

ODD COOKING INSTRUCTIONS

Cooks without clocks and kitchen equipment often improvised. This resulted in some unusual cooking instructions. Among our favourites are directions to crush seeds with a bowling ball and to cook for as long as it takes to say three Lord's Prayers.

Almond Cream Sauce

I am as vigilant as a cat to steal cream.
—1 Henry IV

Cream was a favourite at the Elizabethan table, where it was served in fanciful presentations. Robert May offers more than two dozen recipes for flavoured and thickened creams. Snow Cream was whipped with egg whites and sugar to form a smooth, thick mass to spread over a loaf of bread decorated with a sprig of rosemary to look like an evergreen tree in a snowy field. Cabbage Cream was made by cooking new milk until a layer of skin formed on top, then gathering multiple layers of the rumpled skin and shaping them into a round ball until they resembled a cabbage. Almond Cream is a perfect accompaniment to fruit, pastries, and other desserts.

To make Almond Cream

from *The Accomplisht Cook* by Robert May

Take half a pound of almond paste beaten with rosewater, and strain it with a quart of cream, put it in a skillet with a stick of cinamon and boil it, stir it continually, and when it is boiled thick, put sugar to it, and serve it up cold.

Our Version

1 cup 35% cream
1 cinnamon stick
2 ounces marzipan
2 drops rosewater (optional)

In a small saucepan warm the cream over low heat with the cinnamon stick for about 10 minutes. Stir frequently and do not boil. Break the marzipan into almond-sized pieces. Remove the cinnamon stick and add the marzipan. Continue cooking and stirring until the marzipan is completely dissolved in the cream. Add rosewater, if using. Chill.

Serving Suggestion: Excellent with fresh fruit, apple pie, or cherry custard (see recipe page 182).

From the Frying Pan

Apple Fritters

I think he will carry this island home in his pocket
and give it his son for an apple.
—The Tempest

A delicious variation on the modern donut is made with yeast, the most common raising agent before the invention of baking powder.

BREAKFAST OF CHAMPIONS

Although we might serve apple fritters as a breakfast dish, to the Elizabethans they were strictly dessert fare. Those who ate breakfast usually consumed something "meatier."

In the following exchange from *Antony and Cleopatra,* Enobarbus is asked to confirm rumours of Antony's conspicuous consumption while in Egypt.

Maecenas: Eight wild-boars roasted whole at break-fast, and but twelve persons there; is this true?
Enobarbus: This was but as a fly by an eagle...

cont'd on p. 161

The best fritters

from *The English Housewife* by Gervase Markham

To make the best Fritters, take a pint of creame and warme it; then take eight eggs, only abate fowr of the whites, and beat them well in a dish, and so mixe them with the creame, then put in a little Cloves, Mace, Nutmegge, and Saffron, and stirre them well together; then put in two spoonfull of the best ale-barme, and a little salt, and stirre it again; then make it thick according unto your pleasure with wheate flower; which done, set it within the air of the fire, that it may rise and swell; which when it doth, you shall beate it in once or twice, then put into it a penny pot of sack: all this being done, you shall take a pound or two of very sweet seame, and put it into a panne, and set it over the fire, and when it is molten and begins to bubble, you shall take the fritter batter, and setting it by you, put thicke slices of well-pared Apples into the batter; and then taking the Apples and batter out together with a spoone put it into the boiling seame, and boil your fritters crispe and browne: and when you find the strength of your seame decay, you shall renew it with more seame; and of all sorts of seame that which is made of the beef suet is the best and strongest: when you fritters are made, strow good store of sugar and cinamon upon them, being fair dished, and so serve them up.

Our Version

1 cup table cream or half-and-half cream	1 whole nutmeg, freshly grated (about 1 tablespoon)
1 teaspoon + ¼ cup sugar	¼ teaspoon ground saffron
1 packet rapid-rise yeast	1-½ cups flour, plus extra for dredging
2 eggs	2 tablespoons sherry or liqueur
2 egg yolks	¼ teaspoon salt
½ teaspoon ground cloves	6 firm apples
½ teaspoon ground mace	Oil, for deep-frying

In a small pot warm the cream with the 1 teaspoon of sugar over low heat until it reaches body temperature. Add the yeast and stir gently. Allow the yeast to dissolve and bubble (about 5 minutes). In the meantime, whisk the eggs and egg yolks in a large bowl with the cloves, mace, nutmeg, and saffron. When the yeast and cream mixture is bubbly, whisk it into the egg mixture. Then whisk in the flour. Cover and leave in a warm place for about 40 minutes, or until the mixture is bubbly and has nearly doubled in size.

When the yeast mixture has bubbled up, whisk in the sherry, remaining sugar, and salt. Peel, core, and slice the apples into rings about ½-inch thick. Heat the oil to 180°F. Dredge the apple rings in flour, dip them in batter, and deep-fry until crisp and golden.

After frying you can roll the fritters in a mixture of sugar and cinnamon and eat them like doughnuts or serve them like pancakes with a squirt of lemon juice and a sprinkling of sugar.

A similar report of a prodigious repast occurs in *A Survey of London.*

> **Richard Nevell Earle of Warwicke, with 600 men, all in red jackets imbrodered with ragged staves before and behind, and was lodged in Warwicke Lane: in whose house there was often-times six Oxen eaten at a breakfast, and every Taverne was full of his meate, for he that had aquaintaunce in that house, might have there so much of sodden and rost meate, as hee could pricke and carrie upon a long Dagger.**

The royal breakfast was known to be much more modest. The queen typically would have a glass of beer, along with bread and a piece of beef, in her chambers before officially starting her duties.

French Puffs

Served on toasts like bruschetta, these lemony snacks clear the palate.

To make French Puffes with Greene Hearbes

from *A New Booke of Cookerie* by John Murrell

Take Spinage, Parsley, Endife, a sprigge or two of Savory: mince them very fine: season them with Nutmeg, Ginger, and Sugar. Wet them with Egges, according to the quantitie of the Hearbes, more or lesse. Then take the coare of a Lemmon, cut it in round slices very thinne: put to every slice of your Lemmon one spoonefull of thes stuffe. Then frye it with sweet Lard in a Frying panne as you frye Egges, and serve them with sippets or without, sprinckle them with white Wine or Sacke, or any other Wine, saving Rennish Wine. Serve them eyther at Dinner or Supper.

THE EVILS OF RHENISH WINE

The warning against using Rhenish or Rhine wine on the French puffs seems in keeping with the low opinion of those who drink Rhenish wine in Shakespeare's plays. He portrays them as particularly corrupt and debauched. For example, in *Hamlet,* Claudius, the king of Denmark, murdered his brother, then married the widowed queen to gain the throne and wallow in bouts of drunkenness.

Hamlet: The King doth wake to-night and takes his rouse,
Keeps wassail, and the swagg'ring up-spring reels;
And as he drains his draughts of Rhenish down,
The kettle-drum and trumpet thus bray out
The triumph of his pledge....
This heavy-headed revel east and west
Makes us traduc'd and tax'd of other nations.
They clip us drunkards, and with swinish phrase
Soil our addition, and indeed it takes
From our achievements, though perform'd at height,
The pith and marrow of our attribute.

Our Version

2 eggs
1 cup spinach, cleaned and finely chopped
½ cup parsley, washed and finely chopped
½ cup endive (curly, not Belgian), washed and finely chopped
¼ teaspoon dried savory
¼ teaspoon nutmeg
¼ teaspoon ginger
3 tablespoons sugar
3 lemons
Butter and olive oil, for frying
1 baguette, thinly sliced
White wine

Beat the eggs and then add the chopped greens, seasonings, and sugar. Peel and slice each lemon crosswise into at least 8 slices. Melt the butter with the olive oil to coat a frying pan. Put a spoonful of the mixture on each lemon slice and fry lemon-side-down, spooning oil over the herbs as you fry. Cook until the lemon is very soft and the mixture is cooked (about 5 minutes), then gently spoon each onto a slice of baguette that has been lightly fried in butter. Drizzle a little white wine on top.

Pancakes

Although we like Robert May's pancakes made with cream, many Elizabethan cooks preferred to make them with water in the belief that water would produce a crispier pancake. Some even suggest frying the pancakes twice in order to make them crisp enough "to stand upright."

We prefer our pancakes light and fluffy so we beat the egg whites before folding them into the mixture.

The best pancake

from *The English Housewife* by Gervase Markham

To make the best Pancake, take two or three eggs, and breake them into a dish, and beate them well; then adde unto them a pretty quantity of faire running water, and beate all well together; then put in cloves, mace, cinamon, and a nutmegge, and season it with salt: which done, make it thicke as you think good with fine wheate flour; then fry the cakes as thin as may bee with sweete butter, or sweet seame, and make them brown, and so serve them up with sugar strowed upon them. There be some which mix pancakes with new milk or cream, but that makes them tough, cloying, and not crispe, pleasant and savoury as running water.

PANCAKE TUESDAY

Shrove Tuesday, the day before the start of Lent on Ash Wednesday, was the traditional time to use up butter and eggs in a dish of pancakes, an example of natural pairings given by Lavatch the clown in *All's Well That Ends Well:*

Countess: Will your answer serve fit to all questions?
Clown: As fit as ten groats is for the hand of an attorney, as your French crown for your taffety punk, as Tib's rush for Tom's forefinger, as a pancake for Shrove Tuesday..."

It was tradition to serve the first pancake of the batch (and usually the most soggy, or else burnt) to the last person to make it out of bed as a way of shaming him for his slothful ways.

To make Pancakes

from *The Accomplisht Cook* by Robert May

Take three pints of cream, a quart of flour, eight eggs, three nutmegs, a spoonful of salt, and two pound of clarified butter; the nutmegs being beaten, strain them with the cream, flour and salt, fry them into pancakes and serve them with fine sugar.

Our Version

2 eggs
1-½ cups milk
1 teaspoon nutmeg
¼ teaspoon salt
1 cup flour
Butter and oil, for frying

Separate the eggs and beat the egg whites until stiff. In a separate bowl, blend the milk, egg yolks, nutmeg, and salt. Stir in the flour. Fold in the egg whites. Fry pancakes in oil and butter, turning once. Serve with sugar and lemon juice.

Panperdy

Panperdy is a corruption of the French pain perdu, *meaning lost or stale bread, which can be put to good use to make this flavourful version of what modern cooks have come to know as French toast.*

A SLICE OF BREAD

Falstaff: 'A would have made a good pantler, 'a would 'a chipp'd bread well.

—*2 Henry IV*

In noble houses bread was squared off and the burned bits were cut away by the pantler or "bread-chipper" before it was brought to the table.

Bread was commonly of three types. Manchet, or white bread, was the most prized and expensive, made from fine white flour. Next came the more middle-class Cheat, or wheat bread, which was made from both white and brown flours. Last was Ravelled bread or Pollard made from whole meal and considered to be poor man's food.

To make the best panperdy

from *The English Housewife* by Gervase Markham

To make the best panperdy, take a dozen egges, and breake them, and beat them very well, then put unto them cloves, mace, cinnamon, nutmeg, and good store of sugar, with as much salt as shall season it: then take a manchet, and cut it into thick slices like tostes; which done, take your frying pan, and put into it good store of sweet butter, and, being melted, lay in your slices of bread, then pour upon them one half of your egges; then when that is fried, with a dish turn your slices of bread upward, and then powre on them the other half of your eggs, and so turn them till both sides be brown; then dish it up and serve it with sugar strewed upon it.

Our Version

6 eggs
¼ cup milk
¼ teaspoon ground cloves
¼ teaspoon ground mace
½ teaspoon ground cinnamon
½ teaspoon grated nutmeg
½ cup sugar
Butter, for frying
8 thick slices French bread

In a large bowl beat the eggs with the milk, spices, and sugar until well blended. Heat the butter in a large frying pan and, when it begins to sizzle, arrange the slices of bread in the frying pan. Cook only one layer at a time. Spoon some egg mixture onto each slice of bread, then turn it over and spoon some of the mixture onto the other side. Cook, turning again if necessary, until both sides are golden and the egg mixture is set.

Serving suggestion: Excellent with orange wedges for squeezing, fresh berries, and a sprinkling of sugar.

Quelquechose

According to Gervase Markham "...your fricassees, or quelque-choses,...are dishes of many compositions and ingredients, as flesh, fish, eggs, herbs, and many other things, all being prepared and made ready in a frying pan." The resulting egg dish seasoned with pieces of meat and herbs was an Elizabethan version of the western omelette.

Quelquechose *was contemptuously corrupted into* kickshaws *and used to convey the idea of a mere trifle, as in* Twelfth Night *when foolish Sir Andrew Aguecheek brags about his limited abilities:*

Andrew: ...i'th'world; I am a fellow o' th' strangest mind i'th'world. I delight in masques and revels sometimes altogether.
Toby: Art thou good at these kickshawses, knight?
Andrew: As any man in Illyria, whatsoever he be, under the degree of my betters, and yet I will not compare with an old man.

FOR THE LOVE OF AN EGG

Pandarus: Troilus! why he esteems her no more than I esteem an addle egg.
Cressida: If you love an addle egg as well as you love an idle head, you would eat chickens i' th' shell.

—Troilus and Cressida

EGG INSOLES

Swearing that it "is much used in Italy," the worldly Hugh Platt suggests those with sore feet "put in each sock before he draw on his hose a new laid egge somewhat groselie broken, and so let him travel upon them." As an added bonus, the traveller can use the same cure on his horse.

To fry Eggs

from *The Accomplisht Cook* by Robert May

Take fifteen eggs and beat them in a dish, then have interlarded bacon cut into square bits like dice, and fry them with chopped onions, and put to them cream, nutmeg, cloves cinamon, pepper, and sweet herbs chopped small, (or no herbs nor spice) being fried, serve them on a clean dish, with sugar and juyce of orange.

Our Version

3 rashers bacon, diced
2 green onions, chopped
4 eggs
¼ cup milk
¼ teaspoon ground cloves
¼ teaspoon nutmeg
¼ teaspoon cinnamon
¼ teaspoon pepper
2 tablespoons finely chopped parsley

Fry the bacon until brown, then add the onions. Beat the eggs with the milk, cloves, nutmeg, cinnamon, pepper, and parsley. Drain the excess fat off the bacon, then add the egg mixture and cook gently until the eggs are set.

TANSY

Another popular variation on the omelette theme was Tansy, named for the herb used in fabric dyeing that was the main seasoning along other spring herbs such as violet leaves and green wheat blades.

Sage Fritters

Falstaff: "Seese" and "putter"! Have I liv'd to stand at the taunt of one that makes fritters of English?
—The Merry Wives of Windsor

These little morsels are surprisingly delicious. They're one of our favourite hors d'oeuvres.

To make fritters of Sage and Bay-leaves

from *Epulario* by Giovanne de Rosselli

Take a little fine flower and temper it with Egges, Sugar, Sinamon, Pepper, and a little Saffron to make it yellow, and take whole sage leaves and roule them in this composition one by one, and frie them in Butter or Suet. Do the like with Bayleaves, and in Lent frie them in oyle without Egges and Suet.

NEST EGG

In Shakespeare's day the term *nest egg* referred to an egg left in the nest so as not to disturb the hen when the rest of her eggs were collected. Elizabethan farmers were also advised to pick hens without hind claws that could break the eggs, and to never let a cock set on the eggs since he would crack them and make the hen lose interest. As a special treat for laying hens, one could perfume their nests with sprigs of rosemary.

Our Version

1 egg
1 tablespoon sugar
¼ teaspoon cinnamon
Salt and pepper, to taste
Pinch of ground saffron
¼ cup flour
Butter, for frying
24 fresh sage leaves

Beat the egg with the sugar, cinnamon, salt, pepper, and saffron until smooth. Beat in the flour 1 teaspoon at a time until the batter is the consistency of thick glue and will adhere to the sage leaves.

Melt butter in a frying pan. When it sizzles, fry the battered leaves until they are crispy and golden. Pat dry with a paper towel and serve immediately.

Serving suggestion: Ideal as a snack with beer.

pinach Fritters

How green you are and fresh in this old world!
—King John

Fritters made with fresh greens or fruits could be fried in a yeast batter or simply mixed with a few eggs as in this spinach recipe.

To make Frittors of Spinage

from *The Good Huswifes Handmaide for the Kitchin* attributed to John Partridge

Take a good quantitie of Spinnage, and wash it cleane, and boyle it in faire water, and when it is boyled, put it in a Collender, and let it coole. Then wring all the water out of it as neere as ye can, lay it upon a board, and chop it with the bak of a chopping knife verie smal, and put it in a platter, and put to it four whites of Egs, and two yolks, and the crums of halfe a manchet grated, and a litle Synamon & Ginger, and styrre well together with a spoon and then take a frying pan and a dish of sweete Butter in it, when it is molten put handsomly in your pan halfe a spoonfull of your stuffe, and so bestowe the rest after, fry them on a soft fyre, and turn them when time is, lay them in a platter and cast sugar on them.

MAY DAY, MAY DAY!

Diarist Henry Machin paints this picture of a friendly food fight between two groups of boaters on the Thames: "The furst day of May ther was ii pennys [boats] was deked with stremars, baners and flages, and trumpets and drumes and gones, gahyng a Mayng, and a-ganst the Quens plasse at Westmynster, and ther they shoot and threw eges and orengs on a-gaynst a-nodur, and with sqwybes [firecrackers]."

Unfortunately one of the fire-crackers landed on a bag of gun-powder, which then set "divers men a'fyre." The occupants of the boat rushed to one side, causing it to tip over. Many fell into the Thames, but luckily there were lots of other boats around to help and only one man drowned.

All this occurred under the gaze of Queen Elizabeth I and her lords and ladies from the windows of Westminster.

Our Version

1 10-ounce bag of spinach
2 egg whites
1 egg yolk
½ teaspoon salt
Pinch of cinnamon (optional)
Pinch of ginger (optional)
½ cup bread crumbs
Butter, for frying

GARNISH
Sugar
Lemon wedges

Carefully wash and pick the spinach. Boil the spinach in a minimal amount of water (just enough to cover the bottom of the pot) until tender, about 2 minutes. Drain it well and chop. Beat the egg whites and egg yolk with the salt, cinnamon (if using), and ginger (if using). Mix in the spinach and bread crumbs. If the mixture is too runny, add more crumbs. Fry like pancakes in butter, then serve with sugar and lemon wedges.

From the Orchard

Apples in Puff Pastry

What's this? a sleeve? 'tis like a demi-cannon.
What! up and down carv'd like an apple-tart?
—The Taming of the Shrew

This simple pie is baked flat to best show off its flaky puff pastry. A commercial product gives a fine result and is easy to work with. Boiling the apples in red wine produces the rich colour so valued by Elizabethans.

A quarter Tart of Pippins

from *A New Booke of Cookerie* by John Murrell

Quarter them, and lay them between two sheetes of Paste: put in a piece of whole Sinamon, two or three bruised Cloves, a little sliced Ginger, Orengado, or onely the yellow outside of the Orenge, a bit of Sweet Butter about the bigness of an Egge, good store of Sugar: sprinckle on a little Roewater. Then close your Tart, and bake it: Ice it before it goe to the Boord, serve it hot. This Tart you may make of any puff-paste, or that paste that will not holde the raising. If you bake it in any of these kinds of pastes, then you must first boyle your pippins in Claret Wine and Sugar, or else your Apples will be hard, when your Crust will be burnt and dryed away. Besides, the Wine giveth them a pleasant colour, and a good taste also. Though you boyle your Pippins tender, take heed you breake not the quarters, but bake them whole.

DINING IN STYLE

Hostess Quickly: By this heav'nly ground I tread on, I must be fain to pawn both my plate and the tapestry of my dining-chambers.

Falstaff: Glasses, glasses, is the only drinking, and for thy walls, a pretty slight drollery, or the story of the Prodigal, or a German hunting scene in waterwork, is worth a thousand of these bed-hangers and these fly-bitten tapestries.

—2 Henry IV

Although silver-plated dishes would seem out of place in modern taverns, they were quite common in Elizabethan ones. Once the trend towards elaborate tableware caught on, those with the means replaced their sturdy wooden trenchers and pewter dishes with what Hostess Quickly simply calls "plate." Tapestries used both as wall hangings and as table covers were another decorating must for any "proper" dining room.

cont'd on p. 177

Our Version

6 firm cooking apples, such as Northern Spy	¼ cup sugar
1 14-ounce box commercial puff pastry	1 teaspoon finely grated fresh ginger, or ½ teaspoon ground ginger
1 teaspoon orange zest	2 cinnamon sticks or ½ teaspoon ground cinnamon
¼ teaspoon ground cloves	2 tablespoons butter

For Poaching

¾ cup red wine	½ cup sugar
½ cup water	1 cinnamon stick

Combine the poaching ingredients in a saucepan and bring to a slow boil. Peel the apples, cut them into quarters, and remove the cores. Simmer the apples in the wine mixture. Cook the apples in 2 or 3 batches to ensure they are covered with the wine mixture. Keep the pot covered to prevent evaporation. When the apples turn pink and become soft but not mushy, remove them to a plate and let them cool.

Preheat the oven to 400°F. Roll the pastry into two rectangles, each approximately 10 by 14 inches. Place the first sheet of pastry on a prepared cookie sheet. Arrange the apple quarters on it, leaving a 1-inch margin. Sprinkle the orange zest, cloves, sugar, and ginger on the apples. Lay the cinnamon sticks on top and dot with butter. Wet the margin of the pastry and then lay the top crust over top. Press the edges together and fold them over to prevent the juices from spilling while baking. Bake for about 25 minutes, until the pastry is a rich golden-brown.

Glass drinking vessels were also becoming fashionable during this time, as Falstaff indicates. Since he owes Hostess Quickly a large sum of money, he is probably suggesting she could make do with cheap domestic knock-offs rather than buy pricey Venetian imports. The wall hangings he mentions were painted cloths mimicking tapestries, but not nearly so dear.

Apple Purée

This spiced applesauce is enriched with egg yolks.

SERVING DESSERT

Shallow: Nay, you shall see my orchard, where, in an arbour, we will eat a last year's pippin of mine own grafting, with a dish of caraways, and so forth.

—2 Henry IV

Dessert apples, such as pippins, and caraway seeds were a popular ending to an Elizabethan supper. It was also customary, weather permitting, to move outdoors for this final "banquet," or little meal of desserts, either into one's garden or orchard or into a special "banquetting" house built just for this purpose.

In the manuscript "For to Serve a Lord," servants were given special guidelines on dessert service. First, the supper dishes were cleared and the leftover food scraps were collected in a bowl called a "voider." A fine, clean napkin was laid across the table, and wafers were placed on top. These were accompanied by sweet wine, typically hippocras (see page 212). For special occasions cheese dressed with sugar and sage and seasonal fruits were also presented. In summer these would include strawberries, cherries, pears, and apples. In winter the apples were spiced and roasted, or made into a dish like this apple purée.

To make an Appelmoise

from *A Proper New Booke of Cookery*

Take a dosyn apples, and either roste or boyle them, and draw them throwe a Strayner, and the yolkes of three or foure egges withall, and as ye straine them, temper them with three or foure sponefull of damaske water, if ye will, then take and season it with suger, and halfe a dish of sweete butter, & boyle them upon an chafingdish in a plater, & cast biskets or cinnamon and Ginger, upon them, and so serve them forth.

Our Version

12 apples
½ cup sugar
2 tablespoons butter
1-½ teaspoons ground cinnamon
½ teaspoon ground ginger
A few drops of rosewater (optional)
3 egg yolks, beaten

Preheat the oven to 350°F. Peel and quarter the apples. Put them in a covered casserole dish and bake until soft (about 15 minutes). Purée the apples in a food processor. Stir in the sugar, butter, cinnamon, ginger, rosewater (if using), and egg yolks. Bake uncovered at 250°F for 10 minutes.

Apricot Cream

Go bind thou up yon dangling apricocks,
Which, like unruly children, make their sire
Stoop with oppression of their prodigal weight.
—Richard II

Pairing seasonal fruit with velvety cream was already an established tradition in Shakespeare's day. Ours is a lighter version of Hannah Woolley's recipe, which calls for the apricots to be boiled in cream.

To make Cream Apricoks

from *The Accomplisht Ladys Delight* by Hannah Woolley

First boyl your Apricocks with Water and Sugar, till they are Tender, and afterwards boyl them in Cream, then strain them and season it with Sugar.

Our Version

2 cups dried apricots	Sugar, to taste
1-½ cups white wine	1 cup 35% cream

In a small covered saucepan, cover the apricots with wine and cook them until soft (about 40 minutes). Add sugar to taste. Transfer the mixture to a blender and purée. Let cool. Whip the cream and fold it into the apricot purée.

CREAM FOR THE QUEEN

Entertaining the queen for the weekend enhanced your social standing but put a considerable strain on your wallet. For one such visit in 1561 Sir William and Lady Petre spent in excess of £2500. Among the items purchased were 7 gallons of cream, 200 oranges, and nearly 600 birds (including cygnets, herons, gulls, bitterns, and shoveler ducks).

Baked Melons

Lo, as at English feasts, so I regret
The daintiest last, to make the end most sweet.
—Richard II

In this recipe melons, cucumbers, cabbages, and pumpkins are lumped together as "roots" deemed suitable for stuffing. Forcing, or stuffing, was a common technique used to add flavour and moisture to foods. We've tried to cook squash and cucumbers with variations of this sweet and spicy crumb mixture, as suggested in the original recipe, but it works best with melons.

TO SWEETEN MELONS

Horticulturist Thomas Hill suggests soaking melon and pumpkin seeds in honey and milk before planting to make them sweet. Packing the seeds among rose petals was suggested for floral-tasting fruit.

Forcing for any roots; as Mellons Cucumbers, Collyflowers, Cabbiges, Pompions, Gourds, great Onions, or Parsnips, &c

from *The Accomplisht Cook* by Robert May

Take of Musk-mellon, and take out the seed, and cut it round the mellon two fingers deep, then make a forcing of grated bread, beaten almonds, rose water, and sugar, some musk-mellon stamped small with it, also bisket bread beaten to powder, some coriander seed, candied lemon minced small, some beaten mace and marrow minced small, beaten cinamon, yolks of raw eggs, sweet herbs, saffron, and musk a grain: then fill your rounds of mellons, and put them in a flat bottom'd dish, or earthen pan, with butter in the bottom, and bake them in the dish.

Then have sauce made with white wine and strong broth, strained with beaten almonds, sugar, and cinamon; serve them on sippets finely carved, give this broth a walm, and pour it on your mellons with some fine scraped sugar, dry them in the oven, and so serve them.

Or you may do these whole; mellons, cucumbers lemons, or turnips, and serve them with any boil'd fowls.

Our Version

1 large cantaloupe
Sprigs of fresh mint

STUFFING

½ cup crushed gingersnap cookies
¼ teaspoon ground mace
½ teaspoon ground cinnamon
2 tablespoons chopped fresh mint leaves
2 tablespoons chopped candied lemon peel
2 tablespoons chopped candied ginger

SAUCE

½ cup sweet white wine
2 tablespoons sugar or honey

Cook the wine and sugar or honey together in a small saucepan until reduced by half. Preheat the broiler.

Cut the cantaloupe in quarters, lengthwise, and discard the seeds. Combine the crushed cookies with the mace, cinnamon, mint, lemon peel, and ginger. Spoon a little of the crumb mixture onto each cantaloupe quarter. Arrange the quarters on a baking tray and put them under the broiler for about 4 or 5 minutes. Watch carefully to prevent the crumbs from burning.

To serve, garnish each piece of stuffed cantaloupe with a sprig of fresh mint and drizzle a little of the wine sauce over each quarter.

Cherry Custard

Demetrius: O, how ripe in show
Thy lips, those kissing cherries, tempting grow!
—A Midsummer Night's Dream

We replaced the butter with a little gelatin to glaze this cherry custard, which can be baked with or without a crust.

To make a good tart of Cheries

from *The Good Huswifes Handmaide for the Kitchin* attributed to John Partridge

Take your cheries and pick out the stones of them: then take raw yolks of egs, and put them into your cheries, then take sugar, Sinamon and Ginger, and Cloves, and put to your Cheries + make your Tart with all the Egges, your tart must be of an inche high, when it is made put in your cheries without any liquor, and cast Sugar, Sinamon, and ginger, upon it, and close it up, lay it on a paper, and put it in the Oven, when it is half baken draw it out, and put the liquor that you let of your cheries into the Tart: then take molten butter, and with a feather anoint your lid therewith. Then take a fine beaten Sugar and cast upon it: then put your Tarte into the Oven again, and let it bake a good while, when it is baken draw it foorth, + cast Sugar + Rosewater upon it, and serve it in.

CHOICE CHERRIES

**Helena: ...So we grew together,
Like to a double cherry, seeming parted,
But yet an union in partition,
Two lovely berries moulded on one stem;
So with two seeming bodies, but one heart**

—A Midsummer Night's Dream

Like their modern counterparts, Elizabethan gardeners were always looking for a new variety of plant to furnish their plots. Some of the more unusual varieties of cherry trees available during Shakespeare's day were:

The Great Hungarian Cherry of Zwerts—A prolific fruit-bearer, this tree was said to regularly yield 1 pound of cherries from a single small branch. The fruits, a deep red colour and very sweet, often measured 4 inches around.
cont'd on p. 183

Our Version

1 28-ounce jar cherries	¼ cup sugar
4 egg yolks	¼ teaspoon cinnamon
1 egg	¼ teaspoon ground ginger
½ cup cream	¼ teaspoon ground cloves

TOPPING

Juice from the cherries, approximately 1-¼ cups	2 tablespoons sugar
	1 envelope gelatin

Preheat the oven to 325°F. Arrange the cherries in the bottom of a deep pie dish. Mix the egg yolks, egg, cream, sugar, cinnamon, ginger, and cloves until well blended and pour over the cherries. Bake until the custard is set (approximately 30 minutes). Chill.

In a small saucepan, bring the reserved cherry juice to a boil with the sugar. Remove from the heat and sprinkle the gelatin over the warm liquid. Wait for a minute, then stir until completely dissolved. Cool until syrupy, then ladle the topping over the pie. Chill until set.

The Chameleon or Strange Changeable Cherry—This cherry got its name for two reasons. First, it carried blossoms, unripe fruit, and ripe fruit all at the same time. Second, the fruits were all of different shapes: some were round, some square, and some oblong.

The Urinal Cherry—As one might expect, the cherries from this tree were shaped like miniature urinals. It was not, however, to be confused with the Long Finger Cherry.

reamed Codling Pie

Not yet old enough for a man, nor young enough for a boy; as a squash is before 'tis a Peascod, or a codling when 'tis almost an apple.
—Twelfth Night

Codlings are young green apples, picked before maturity. When sweetened with sugar and enriched with cream, they make a luscious pie filling.

THE PIE THAT COULDN'T GET A DATE

Markham's instruction to add one date to the apple pie filling seems odd, but to Elizabethans a pie without a date simply wasn't a pie, as evidenced by this passage from *Troilus and Cressida:*

Pandarus: ...Is not birth, beauty, good shape, discourse, manhood, learning, gentleness, virtue, youth, liberality, and such-like, the spice and salt that season a man?
Cressida: Ay, a minc'd man, and then to be bak'd with no date in the pie, for then the man's date is out.

A Codling Pie

from *The English Housewife* by Gervase Markham

Take Codlins as before-said; and pill them, and divide them in halfes, and chore them, and lay a leare thereof in the bottom of the pie: then scatter here and there a clove, and here and there a peece of whole cinamon; then cover them all over with suger, then lay another leare of codlings, and doe as before said, and so another, till the coffin be all filled; then cover all with Suger, and here and there a Clove and Cinamon stick, and if you will a slic't orange pill and a date; then cover it, and bake it as the pies of that nature: when it is bak't, draw it out of the oven, and take of the thickest and best Creame with good store of Suger, and give it one boil or two on the fire: then open the pie, and put the Creame therein, and mash the codlins all about: then cover it, and having trimd the lid (as was before showed in the like pies and tarts), set it into the oven again for half an hour, and so serve it forth.

Our Version

5–6 apples, preferably a tart variety such as Granny Smith
3 small cinnamon sticks
4 cloves
¾ cup brown sugar
½ teaspoon orange zest
1 date (optional)
Flaky pastry for a covered 9-inch pie (see recipe page 124)
½ cup 35% cream

Preheat oven to 350°F. Peel, core, and slice apples. Place them in a casserole dish with the cinnamon, cloves, brown sugar, orange zest, and date. Cover and bake for about 30 minutes, or until apples are soft.

Once apples are cooked, leave the dish uncovered to cool. Remove the cloves and cinnamon sticks. Roll out the pastry and line a 9-inch pie plate. Increase the heat of the oven to 375°F. Mash the apple mixture until smooth, then pour in the cream and blend until smooth. Fill the pie shell, cover, and cut vents. Bake for about 30 minutes, until the crust is golden-brown.

SHOPPING LIST FOR A SHEEP SHEARING FESTIVAL

Clown: I must have saffron to colour the warden pies; mace; dates, none—that's out of my note; nutmegs, seven: a race or two of ginger, but that I may beg; four pounds of pruins, and as many of raisins o' th' sun.

—The Winter's Tale

Pear Pie

Falstaff: I warrant they would whip me with their fine wits till I were as crestfall'n as a dried pear.
—The Merry Wives of Windsor

Elizabethan cooks began this recipe by poaching the pears in thick syrup in a dough-covered dish in the oven, a step that modern cooks can skip by simply using canned pears. The dough used to cover the poaching dish was not the final pie crust but a covering that would have sealed in the juices and prevented smoke from spoiling the taste of the fruit.

To Make a Warden or Pear-pye

from *The Accomplisht Ladys Delight* by Hannah Woolley

Bake your Wardens or Pears in an Oven with a little Water, and a good quantity of Sugar; let your Pot be covered with a piece of Dough; let them not be fully baked for a quarter of an hour, when they are cold make a high Coffin, and put them in whole, adding to them some Cloves, whole Cinamon, Sugar, with some of the Liquor they were baked in, so bake it.

Our Version

2 28-ounce cans pear halves (preferably packed in their own juice)	Flaky pastry for a covered 9-inch pie (see recipe page 124)
6 whole cloves	Ground cinnamon, to taste (about 1 teaspoon)
1 cinnamon stick	1 egg, beaten
½ cup sugar	Sugar, for topping

Drain the pears and save the juice from 1 can. Boil the reserved juice with the whole cloves, cinnamon stick, and sugar until the mixture is reduced to approximately one-quarter of its original volume.

Preheat the oven to 375°F. Roll out the pastry and line a 9-inch pie plate. Arrange the pears in the pastry and sprinkle with ground cinnamon. Pour the boiled juice mixture over them. Cover the pie and make slits in top layer of pastry for steam to escape. Brush with beaten egg and sprinkle with sugar. Bake for 30 minutes.

Optional decoration: Shape scraps of leftover pastry into small pears, using cloves as stems. These can be stuck on the pie with a little beaten egg.

PLENTY OF PEARS

Pears were a standard feature in Elizabethan orchards. Although Shakespeare mentions only the Warden and the Poprin pear, there were dozens of others, including the Bon Chretien, Summer Bergamot, Duetete or double-headed pear, Geneting, Norwich, Rowling, Turnep, Hawkesbill, and Slipper. The Hundred Pound pear earned its name not for any attribute of the fruit, but for the cost of obtaining a graft.

Prune Tart

The mellow plum doth fall, the green sticks fast,
Or being early pluck'd, is sour to taste.
—Venus and Adonis

We combined the best of two recipes to produce a smooth, sweet purée to fill this tart.

To make a tart of Prunes

from *A Proper New Booke of Cookery*

Take Prunes and set them by on a chafer with a little red wine, and put therto a manchet and let them boyle together then draw them throw a strainer, with the yokes of iiii egges, and season it with suger, and so bake it.

To make a Damson tart

from *The Accomplisht Ladys Delight* by Hannah Woolley

Take Damsons and seethe them in Wine and strain them with a little cream, then boyl your stuff over the fire till it be thick, and put thereto Sugar, Cinamon and Ginger. But set it not in the Oven after; but let your paste be baked before.

EAU D'ELIZABETHAN

To put it mildly, Shakespeare's world was heavily scented. One writer complains that the typical household floor was a filthy jumble of spilled beer, grease, bone fragments, spittle, and dog urine, covered by a layer of rushes. Elizabethans masked the bad odours that they associated with the plague by using pomanders, nosegays, strewing herbs, and sweet powders for linens and clothes. In *Much Ado About Nothing* Borachio poses as "a perfumer,...smoking a musty room..." by burning mixtures of herbs and spice. Cookbooks listed recipes for these "fumigations," which typically contained marjoram, sandalwood, ample quantities of roses, and sometimes even laudanum.

Our Version

Sweet pastry (see recipe page 124)
1 cup prunes
½ cup red wine
¼ cup water
1 cinnamon stick
¼ cup cream, preferably 35%
¼ cup sugar
¼ teaspoon ground cinnamon
¼ teaspoon ground ginger

Preheat oven to 350°F. Roll out pastry and line a tart pan. Prick pastry all over with a fork to prevent it from rising and bubbling when it bakes. Bake until golden, about 20 minutes.

Meanwhile, place the prunes in a saucepan with the wine, water, and cinnamon stick. Cover and cook over low heat until the prunes have absorbed most of the moisture, about 25 minutes. Remove the cinnamon stick. Purée the prunes and any remaining cooking liquid in a food processor. Stir in cream, sugar, ground cinnamon, and ginger. Pour into the baked tart crust.

CRIME AND PUNISHMENT

In 1552 a fruit seller named Greg stuffed fern leaves in the bottom of pots of strawberries and tried to pass them off as full measures in Southwarke. His punishment was the pillory.

Strawberry Tart

Bishop of Ely: The strawberry grows underneath the nettle,
And wholesome berries thrive and ripen best
Neighbour'd by fruit of baser quality.
—Henry V

Red wine enhances the flavour of the strawberries in this quick and simple tart.

To make a tarte of Strawberries

from *The Good Huswifes Jewell* by Thomas Dawson

Wash your strawberies, and put them into your Tarte, and season them with suger, cynamon and Ginger, and put in a little red wine into them.

Our Version

Sweet pastry for 9-inch pie (see recipe page 124) or commercially prepared pie dough	½ cup sugar
4 cups strawberries, washed, hulled, and quartered	¼ teaspoon cinnamon
	¼ teaspoon ginger
	¼ cup red wine
	2 tablespoons cornstarch

Preheat the oven to 350°F. Roll out the pastry and line a 9-inch pie plate. Bake the crust blind (or empty). To ensure that the pastry keeps its shape, prick it all over with a fork. Bake until the pastry is golden (about 20 minutes), then remove from the oven.

While the pastry is baking, prepare the filling. Put the strawberries in a saucepan with the sugar, cinnamon, ginger, and half of the wine. Simmer for 10 minutes. Bring to a boil. Mix the cornstarch with the remaining wine until it is fully dissolved. Pour the cornstarch mixture into the strawberries and stir well until thickened. Remove from the heat. Fill the tart shell.

Sweet Endings

TOOLS OF THE TRADE

Beating egg whites was a particularly laborious task without metal whisks. Elizabethan cooks were instructed to beat their egg whites with a few goose feathers tied together or with a wooden stick split into four pieces at one end, or to repeatedly squeeze them through a sea sponge.

DAINTIES AND SUBTLETIES

Almonds appear in numerous Elizabethan recipes as a thickening agent and a sweetener. One of their most popular uses was for "marchpane," or marzipan. No special event or large feast was considered complete without a "subtlety" or confection fashioned from either "marchpane" or a sugar plate made of sugar, rosewater, and gum draganth (also known as Arabic gum).

cont'd on p. 195

Almond Macaroons

The parrot will not do more for an almond than he for a commodious drab.
—Troilus and Cressida

These chewy macaroons are made with ground almonds instead of coconut. To prevent them from sticking to the pan, Elizabethan cooks were instructed to bake their macaroons on wafers, crisp waffle-like cookies. Modern cooks may bake the macaroons either on circles of edible rice paper or on sheets of parchment paper to prevent them from sticking to the cookie sheet.

To make Mackrons

from *The Accomplisht Ladys Delight* by Hannah Woolley

Take Almonds, Blanch them, Beat them in a Morter, with Serced Sugar mingled therewith, with the white of an Egg and Rose-water, then Beat them altogether till they are as thick as Fritters, then Drop it upon your Wafers and Bake it.

Our Version

1-¼ cups ground almonds	2 egg whites
¾ cup sugar	2 drops rosewater or vanilla
1 teaspoon all-purpose flour	

Preheat the oven to 350°F. Mix the ground almonds, sugar, and flour in a large bowl. Beat the egg whites until they form peaks and then fold them into the almond mixture with the rosewater or vanilla. Drop by spoonfuls onto a baking sheet lined with parchment and bake in preheated oven until puffy and firm (about 20 minutes). Makes 2 dozen macaroons.

Variation: Substitute 1-¼ cups ground hazelnuts for the ground almonds and use vanilla instead of rosewater for a richer, nuttier flavour.

Serving suggestion: Serve with fresh fruits, especially cherries, at the end of a meal. The hazelnut macaroons are delicious with apricot cream (see recipe page 179).

Molds of wood, plaster, or tin were used to shape frogs, rabbits, snails, and birds. Household items included buttons, keys, shoes, and gloves. Those who wanted to go all out could furnish their entire table with sugar plate dishes to be eaten at the end of the meal.

Recreating food in sugar pastes was also fashionable, and cookbooks listed instructions for using small birch twigs to simulate cherry stalks and dredging the bird shapes in bread crumbs and cinnamon to make them look as if they had been roasted. In this manner, one author suggests that a dessert course might "bee presented in the forme of a supper, being a verie rare and strange device." In addition to the brown tone achieved by the use of cinnamon, a variety of colours could be made: yellow from saffron, orange from marigolds, red from turnsole, and blue from violets.

SHAKESPEARE'S CULINARY CHARACTERS

- Robin Starveling
- Peaseblossom
- Mustardseed
- Costard
- Dogberry
- Sir Toby Belch
- Slender
- Froth
- Mistress Overdone

Aniseed Cake

Dost thou think because thou art virtuous there
shall be no more cakes and ale?
—Twelfth Night

The original recipe produces a dense, very sweet, and intensely anise-flavoured loaf. The stiff dough was shaped in rings and turned over halfway through baking. We've provided both the traditional version and a much lighter variation.

Fine bread

from *The English Housewife* by Gervase Markham

Take a quarter of a pound of fine suger well beaten, and as much flower finely boulted, with quantitie of Aniseeds a little bruised, and mingle all together; then take two egges and beate them very well, whites and all; then put in the mingled stuffe aforesaid, and beat all together a good while, then put it into a mould, wiping the bottom ever first with butter to make it come out easily, and in the baking turne it once or twice as you shall have occasion, and so serve it whole, or in slices at your pleasure.

Our Version

2 eggs, separated
⅔ cup sugar
1 cup flour
3 tablespoons aniseed, lightly crushed

Preheat the oven to 325°F. Beat the egg yolks with the sugar until the mixture is pale yellow. Beat the egg whites until stiff. Stir the flour and aniseed into the egg yolk mixture. Stir in the egg whites. Spread the mixture into a small (6 inch), prepared cake tin.

Bake at 325°F for about 40 minutes, or until golden.

Variation: For a lighter, softer cake, increase the eggs to 4.

Jumbles

More are men's ends mark'd than their lives before.
The setting sun, and the music at the close,
As the last taste of sweets, is sweetest last,
Writ in remembrance more than things long past.
—Richard II

These crunchy, aniseed-flavoured cookies are a tasty addition to the banquet or dessert table. We've reduced the recipe to make about three dozen "jumbles."

To make Jombils a hundred

from *The Good Huswifes Jewell* by Thomas Dawson

Take twenty Egges and put them into a pot both the yolkes & the white, beat them wel, then take a pound of beaten sugar and put to them, and stirre them wel together, then put to it a quarter of a peck of flower, and make a hard paste thereof, and then with anniseeds mould it well, and make it in little rowles beeing long, and tye them in knots, and wet the ends in Rosewater, then put them into a pan, but even in one waum, then take them out with a skimmer and lay them in a clothe to drie, this doon lay them in a tart panne, the bottom being oyled, then put them into a temperate Oven for one howre, turning them often in the oven.

GINGERBREAD

Elizabethans munched on several types of "cookies" we still enjoy today, including biscotti and gingerbread. Their version of gingerbread differed in taste and texture from our own, as it was made from bread crumbs boiled in wine with honey, ginger, and other spices.

And I had but one penny in the world, thou shouldst have it to buy gingerbread.

—Loves's Labour's Lost

Our Version

2 eggs
½ cup sugar
3 teaspoons aniseed
1-½ cups flour
Rosewater or liqueur (optional)

Beat the eggs for 2 minutes until frothy. Beat in sugar, then aniseed and flour. If the dough is too sticky to work with, add a little more flour. Roll the dough into long ropes about ½-inch thick. Cut into 3- to 4-inch lengths and tie each piece into a knot. Preheat the oven to 300°F.

Boil a large pot of water, then drop the knots into the water and boil until they rise to the surface (2 minutes or less). Remove from the water and drain. Arrange on a prepared cookie sheet. Brush with rosewater or liqueur (if using), then bake in the oven for about 50 minutes, or until golden.

Serving suggestion: Serve with buttered beer (see page 210) for dipping.

Claret Jelly

...distill'd
Almost to jelly with the act of fear,
—Hamlet

This recipe illustrates the arduous process of making gelatin by boiling animal hooves to extract the glutinous material, then repeatedly straining the liquid through sieves and jelly bags to remove any impurities. The egg whites caught the smallest particles and solidified them before they could trickle through the bag. Issinglass, a form of gelatin derived from sturgeons' bladders, helped set the broth. Turnsole is a red colouring derived from flowers. Without a little extra colour the wine gelatin tends to look grey. Modern cooks can take advantage of labour-saving instant gelatin, as well as more convenient molds. Elizabethan cooks used scallop, cockle, or mussel shells, eggshells, or hollowed-out half-lemons.

TOO SWEET A TOOTH

Troilus: But still sweet love is food for fortune's tooth.

—*Troilus and Cressida*

The Elizabethans' love of sweets led to tooth decay in the mouths of those who could afford to eat them. Queen Elizabeth I herself had teeth blackened with rot, "A defect," one writer notes, "the English seem subject to, from their too great use of sugar."

Even the tooth cleansers of the time were often loaded with sweeteners such as honey. Small wonder then that there were just as many recipes for toothache cures as there were for cleaning compounds. For really tough jobs people went to the barber to have their teeth scaled.

If all else failed, you could seek the services of a tooth-drawer. Queen Elizabeth I was apparently terrified of having her teeth pulled, even if they caused her tremendous pain. At one point a member of her court had his own perfectly healthy tooth pulled in front of her to convince her that it was painless.

To make Jelly

from *A Book of Cookrye* by A.W.

Take Calves feete and fley them, and faire washe them, and set them on to seethe in faire licour, and faire scum them, and when they be tender sod, faire straine out the licour, and see your licour be verye cleere, and put your licour into a pot, if there be a pottle of it, put a pottle of claret wine unto it, and two pound Sugar, a quartern of sinamon, half a quartern of ginger, an ounce of Nutmegs, an ounce of grains, some long Pepper, a fewe Cloves whole, a few Coriander seeds, a little salt, Isonglasse being faire washed and laid in water a day before, Turnsole being aired by the fire and dulled, and when they be wel sod, let it ron through a bag, and put two whites of Egs in the bag.

Our Version

2 cups red wine
2 cups water
½ cup sugar
2 cinnamon sticks
1-inch piece fresh ginger, peeled
2 nutmegs, cut in half
Few drops of vanilla
Red food colouring
2 packets instant gelatin
2 egg whites and crushed eggshells

In stainless steel or enamel pot, simmer wine with water, sugar, cinnamon sticks, ginger, nutmeg, and vanilla. Remove from heat. Add food colouring. Sprinkle gelatin on warm liquid. When melted, stir well.

Combine egg whites and crushed shells, then put them into the warm jelly mixture while whisking rapidly. Return the mixture to the heat until it boils, then remove from the heat and wait for boiling to subside. This allows the sediment to bubble up into the foamy egg whites, where it is trapped. Return to the heat and bring to a boil twice more.

Strain the liquid very slowly through a sieve lined with a large paper coffee filter or multiple layers of cheesecloth while holding back the egg foam. Try not to break the egg foam. This is a slow process that cannot be hurried. If the jelly starts to set, return it to the heat until it liquefies. Pour into wet molds and refrigerate. Just before serving, dip the molds in a bowl of hot water for a few seconds to loosen the jelly, then invert onto a serving plate.

Serving suggestion: Garnish with citrus slices and serve as a light dessert or as a refreshing interlude between two heavy courses. Excellent with rice pudding (see recipe page 152).

A MOON HALF EMPTY OR HALF FULL?

In *The Jewell House of Art and Nature* Hugh Platt seems to describe the gravitational effect of the moon on oceans and a method to recreate this in microcosm: "It hath beene crediblie reported unto me, that if an ordinarie drinking glasse be filled brim full, a little before the full of the Moone, that, even at that instant when the Moone commeth to the full, the water will presently boile over."

oonshine Eggs

Kent: ...Draw, you rogue, for though it be night,
yet the moon shines; [drawing his sword] I'll make a
sop o' th' moonshine of you, you whoreson cullionly
barber-monger, draw!
—KING LEAR

Poached egg yolks make a fanciful dish of miniature "moons" for the dessert table. The instruction to use a full dish of rosewater doesn't work with commercial rosewater, which is often artificially flavoured. To avoid eating something that tastes like perfume we suggest using rosewater in minute quantities.

To make egges in mone shine

from *A Proper New Booke of Cookery*

Take a dishe of rosewater, and a dish full of suger, and set them upon a chafing dish, and let them boile, then take the yokes of 8 or 9 egges newlaid, and put them therto, every one from other, and so let them harden a little, and so after this maner serve them forth, and cast a little Cinnamon and suger.

Our Version

1 cup water
2 drops rosewater
¾ cup sugar
6 egg yolks
¼ cup sugar
Pinch of cinnamon

Combine the water, rosewater, and ¾ cup sugar in a small saucepan and bring to a gentle boil. Carefully separate all of the white from the egg yolks. Gently lower the yolks into this liquid, one at a time, and cook them until firm (about 3 minutes each).

Arrange the cooked egg yolks on a small serving plate and sprinkle with remaining sugar and cinnamon.

Orange Comfits

From violet leaves to fennel seeds, the Elizabethans candied just about everything imaginable, including the always-popular orange peel. These candies, or kissing comfits as they were called, became the breath mints of the age. And demand for them remained high since so many people suffered from gum disease and rotten teeth.

Some comfit recipes call for several separate coatings of sugar, which would produce a hard outer layer. By contrast, our comfits are moist and slightly chewy with a delightful hint of wine.

To make Orenge Comfets

from *The Treasurie of Hidden Secrets* by John Partridge

Take Orenge pillings, lay them in faire water a day and night, then seeth them in white Wine: then take them out of the Wine, and put them in an earthen pot, & put therein Suger, Cinamon, Cloves, and Mace whole, and seeth them together without any other liquor, and so it is made.

STAGE HAIL

Falstaff: ...Let the sky rain potatoes; let it thunder to the tune of "Green-sleeves," hail kissing-comfits, and snow eringoes; let there come a tempest of provocation, I will shelter me here.

—*The Merry Wives of Windsor*

Twenty years before Shakespeare wrote these lines another theatrical mind beat him to the concept of a candy storm. Holinshed describes a masque held for a visiting dignitary in his *Chronicles of England*. The tragic play was a narration of the destruction of Troy and featured a "tempest wherein it hailed small confects, rained rosewater, and snew an artificial kind of snow, all strange, marvellous and abundant."

Our Version

- 1-½ cups diced orange peel (skins from approximately 6 oranges)
- 1-½ cups white wine
- 1 cinnamon stick
- 12 whole cloves
- ½ teaspoon mace
- ¾ cup sugar

Soak the orange peel overnight in water before dicing it into ¼-inch squares. In a saucepan, bring the wine to a boil and add the spices and orange peel. Reduce the heat and simmer for about 45 minutes, stirring occasionally. Remove from heat. Strain and pick out spices. Reserve the liquid.

In a separate pot, dissolve the sugar in 2 tablespoons of the reserved liquid. When the sugar is completely dissolved, raise the heat and bring to a boil. Remove from heat, add orange peel, and stir well to ensure an even coating. Spoon onto a cookie sheet and let dry.

Banbury Cakes

These delicious currant-filled pastries can easily be made with commercially prepared puff pastry instead of the yeast dough that Markham suggests needs "working for an hour or more."

REGIONAL CUISINE

Banbury cakes, named for the Oxfordshire market town, exemplify the regional cuisine of Shakespeare's day. Lancashire has its own version of the currant-filled pastry: the eccles cake.

Counties and towns each produced distinctive cheeses. Banbury was known for its particularly thin variety, which Bardolph uses to insult Master Slender in *The Merry Wives of Windsor:* "You Banbury cheese!"

To make a Banbury cake

from *The English Houswife* by Gervase Markham

To make a very good Banbury Cake, take 4 pounds of Currants, and wash and picke them very cleane, and drie them in a cloth: then take three egges and put away one yolke, and beat them, and straine them with good barme, putting thereto Cloves, Mace, Cinamon and Nutmegges; then take a pint of creame, and as much mornings milk and set it on the fire til the cold be taken away; then take flour and put in good store of cold butter and sugar, then put in your egges, barme and meale and work them all together an hour or more; then save a part of the Past, and the rest break in peeces and work in your Currants; which done, mould your Cake of what quantity you please; and then with that past which hath not any currants cover it very thin both underneath and a loft. And so bake it according to the bignesse.

Our Version

⅓ cup butter
⅓ cup brown sugar
1 egg
1-½ cups currants, washed and picked
½ cup candied orange peel
¼ cup ground almonds
½ teaspoon grated nutmeg
½ teaspoon ground cinnamon
¼ teaspoon ground cloves
¼ teaspoon ground mace
14 ounces puff pastry
Milk and sugar, to finish

Preheat the oven to 400°F.

Cream the butter and brown sugar. Beat in the egg, then the currants, orange peel, almonds, nutmeg, cinnamon, cloves, and mace.

Roll the puff pastry out thinly, then using a small bowl or saucer as a template, cut out circles approximately 5 inches in diameter. You should end up with 14 to 15 circles if you roll the scraps together.

Place roughly 2 tablespoons of filling in the centre of each pastry circle, then brush the edges with a little milk. Gather the edges together until they overlap and gently pat them to seal. Place gathered side down on a prepared baking sheet. Cut a little slit in the top of each cake, then brush with milk and sprinkle with sugar.

Bake until the pastry is golden-brown, about 25 to 30 minutes.

To Slake the Thirst

Buttered Beer

And here's a pot of good double-beer, neighbour.
—2 Henry VI

This unusual-sounding beverage makes a warming drink for a winter evening. It's a delightful alternative to eggnog or mulled wine. Double beer was a particularly potent brew.

To make Buttered Beere

from *The Good Huswifes Handmaide for the Kitchin* attributed to John Partridge

Take three pintes of Beere, put five yokes of Egges to it, straine them together, and set it in a pewter pot to the fyre, and put to it halfe a pound of Sugar, one penniworth of Nutmegs beaten, one penniworth of Cloves beaten, and a halfepenniworth of Ginger beaten, and when it is all in, take another pewter pot and brewe them together, and set it to the fire againe, and when it is readie to boyle, take it from the fire, and put a dish of sweet butter into it, and brewe them together out of one pot into an other.

MY BEER'S BETTER THAN YOUR BEER

Even in Queen Elizabeth I's time, English beer had an international reputation for excellence. One writer notes, "English Beere is famous in Netherland and lower Germany, which is made of Barley and Hops; for England yeelds plenty of Hops, howsoever they also use Flemish Hops. The Cities of lower Germany upon the sea forbid the publike selling of English Beere, to satisfie their own brewers, but privately swallow it like Nectar."

Our Version

½ cup sugar
½ teaspoon grated nutmeg
½ teaspoon ground cloves
¼ teaspoon ground ginger
2 egg yolks
1 pint ale or dark beer
2 tablespoons melted butter

Mix the sugar, spices, and egg yolks in a small bowl. Warm the beer slowly in a stainless steel bowl over a saucepan filled with water on low heat. Whisk in the sugar mixture, then the butter. Be careful not to overheat or overcook.

Hippocras

Rosaline: I would thou couldst stammer, that thou mightest pour this conceal'd man out of thy mouth, as wine comes out of a narrow-mouth'd bottle, either too much at once, or none at all. I prithee, take the cork out of thy mouth that I may drink thy tidings.
—As You Like It

Hippocras, or spiced wine, was served at special occasions such as weddings and christenings. Sweet and spicy, it resembles a liqueur.

To make Epocras

from *The English Housewife* by Gervase Markham

Take a gallon of Clarret-wine, and put therin foure ounces of Ginger, an ounce and a halfe of Nutmegs, Of cloves one quarter, of Suger foure pound; let all this stand together in a pot at least twelve houres, then take it, and put it into a cleane bagge made for the purpose, so that the wine may come with good leasure from the spices.

CALLING FOR CUPS

Cups were commonly kept on the sideboard during meals and called for when a diner was thirsty. The servant would bring the refreshment, let the person drink, then wipe the cup clean and return it to its place.

During the sixteenth century, wood, leather, and pewter tankards and cups were gradually replaced by more elegant vessels of silver, gold, and glass. Some of the more exotic cup-making materials included ostrich eggs, coconut shell, and alabaster.

Come, thou monarch of the vine,
Plumpy Bacchus with pink eyne!
In thy vats our cares be drown'd,
With thy grapes our hairs be crown'd!
Cup us till the world go round,
Cup us till the world go round!

—Antony and Cleopatra

Our Version

1 25-ounce bottle dry white wine	2 nutmegs, cut in quarters
1-inch piece fresh ginger, peeled and sliced	5 cloves
	1-½ cups sugar

Combine all of the ingredients in a large glass jar. Leave covered for 2 or 3 days, then strain through a paper coffee filter to clarify.

NON-TOXIC TANKARDS

Elizabethans believed that they could poison-proof drinking vessels by lining them with such "poison-alerting" materials as narwhale horn, rhinoceros horn, rock crystal, agate, and serpentine. All were said to change colour if exposed to toxic substances.

Posset

Robert May offers half a dozen different ways to make this rich, creamy drink, which was a popular fortifier in Shakespeare's day. Variations include adding nutmeg as well as cinnamon to season the thickened "curd." Serve this thick, custard-like drink in small punch cups with spoons.

POSSET NIGHTCAP

Mistress Quickly tells us in *The Merry Wives of Windsor* that posset was usually consumed as a calming bedtime drink—the Elizabethan equivalent of curling up with a cup of cocoa: "Go, and we'll have a posset for 't soon at night, in faith at the latter end of a sea-coal fire."

To make a Posset

from *The Accomplisht Cook* by Robert May

Take the yolks of twenty eggs, then have a pottle of good thick sweet cream, boil it with good store of whole cinamon, and stir it continually on a good fire, then strain the eggs with a little raw cream when the cream is well boiled and tasteth of the spice, take it off the fire, put in the eggs, and stir them well in the cream, being pretty thick, have some sack in a posset pot or deep silver bason, half a pound of double refined sugar, and some fine grated nutmeg, warm it in the bason and pour it as high as you can hold the skillet, let it spatter in the bason to make it froth, it will make a most excellent posset; then have loaf sugar finely beaten, and strow on it good store.

To the curd you may adde some fine grated manchet, some claret or white wine, or ale onely.

Our Version

¾ cup 35% cream	¼ cup sugar
2 cinnamon sticks	¼ teaspoon grated nutmeg
½ cup sherry	4 egg yolks

Warm the cream with the cinnamon sticks for 15 minutes over low heat. Do not boil. In a stainless steel bowl set over a saucepan of water on low heat, warm the sherry with the sugar and nutmeg.

Remove the cream from the heat and discard the cinnamon sticks. Beat the egg yolks and stir in the warm cream a little at a time. Pour the egg and cream mixture into the sherry and whisk it until smooth and thick. Sprinkle with nutmeg.

Low heat and constant stirring are essential to prevent this dish from turning into scrambled eggs.

Glossary

ambergreese, or ambergris An odoriferous secretion produced by sperm whales
barberry *Barberea vulgaris,* a sour-tasting, edible berry
barm Yeast
bolt To sift
borage *Borago officinalis,* an herb used in salads and cordials
bray To beat or grind into powder
broom An herb used in dyeing
bugloss Various plants of the genus *Anchusa* with large hairy leaves
burdock, or burr A plant of the genus *Arctium;* a wild plant whose root is reputed to have medicinal properties
capon Castrated fowl
carbonado To grill meat over coals
caudle A warm, seasoned drink of thickened wine
charger A platter
cheat Bread made with a combination of white and whole wheat flour
claret A dry, red wine from the Bordeaux district of France
codling An unripe apple
colewort A cabbage or other plant from the *brassica* family
collop A small slice
cony A rabbit
doucet A custard pie
endive *Cichorium endivia,* a salad herb
farce To stuff, or a filling for roast meat or fowl
galantine A sauce thickened with blood
gammon A hindquarter of cured pork (ham or bacon)
gigot A leg
graine A miniscule measurement of weight equal to 1/20 scruple
hippocras A sweetened and spiced wine
hyssop *Hyssopus officinalis,* an aromatic herb

issinglass Gelatin obtained from sturgeon
kickshaw A corruption of *quelquechose*
langdebeef From *langue de boeuf,* ox tongue; see bugloss
marchpane A decorated cake of marzipan
muscadine A sweet wine
olive Thin slice of meat
panperdy From *pain perdu,* lost bread, bread dipped in egg and fried
pennyroyal *Mentha pulegium,* a strongly scented variety of mint
pettitoes Pig's trotters
pipken An earthenware pot
pippin A superior-quality apple
posset A hot drink of sack thickened with cream
pottle Two quarts
quelquechose A composite dish containing many different ingredients
rocket Roquette, *Eruca vesicaria sativa,* arugula, a salad herb
sack A wine similar to sherry
sanders Sandalwood, an aromatic wood used for colouring
scruple A small unit of weight equal to 1/24 ounce
seam Clarified animal fat
searce To sift
sippet A small slice of toast or fried bread
skirret A variety of parsnip
sop A large piece of bread served with pottages and stews
succory *Cichorium intybus,* a wild plant eaten young as a salad herb
sucket A piece of fruit or vegetable preserved in syrup
sward Rind
tansy *Tanacetum vulgare,* an aromatic herb used in dying fabric; also a dish containing composite herbs
trencher A large wooden plate or platter
turnsole *Chorzophoria tinctoria,* a plant used for deep-red food colouring
verjuice Sour crabapple juice
walm Boil
warden A cooking pear
wort An herbaceous plant or pot-herb, or malt infusion used to brew beer

Bibliography

Brett, Gerrard. *Dinner Is Served: A History of Dining in England.* London: Hart-Davis, 1968.

Burton, Elizabeth. *The Elizabethans at Home.* London: Secker & Warburg, 1958.

Byrne, M. St. Clare. *Elizabethan Life in Town and Country.* Norfolk: Cox & Wyman Ltd, 1961.

Drummond, Jack. *The Englishman's Food—A History of Five Centuries of English Diet.* London: Reader's Union, Jonathan Cape, 1959.

Emmison, F.G. *Tudor Food and Pastimes.* London: Ernest Benn Ltd., 1964.

Evans, G. Blakemore (ed.). *The Riverside Shakespeare.* Boston: Houghton Mifflin Company, 1974.

Harbage, Alfred. *Shakespeare's Audience.* New York: Columbia University Press, 1958.

Harrison, Molly. *The Kitchen in History.* London: Osprey Publishers Ltd., 1972.

Hibbert, Christopher. *The English, A Social History.* London: Paladin Grafton Books, 1988.

Holden, Anthony. *William Shakespeare.* London: Little, Brown and Company, 1999.

Oxford, Arnold. *English Cookery Books to the Year 1850.* London: Henry Frowde, 1913.

Paston-Williams, Sara. *The Art of Dining: A History of Cooking and Eating.* London: National Trust, 1993.

Quayle, Eric. *Old Cookbooks: An Illustrated History.* New York: Dutton, 1978.

Sass, Lorna J. *To the Queen's Taste: Elizabethan Feasts and Recipes.* New York: Metropolitan Museum of Art, 1976.

Willan, Anne. *Great Cooks and Their Recipes.* London: McGraw-Hill Book Company Limited, 1977

Period Works

Elyot, Thomas. *The Castel of Helth (1541).* London: Scholar's Facsimiles & Reprints.

Furnivall, Frederick J., ed. *Early English Meals and Manners.* Detroit: Singing Tree Press, 1969 (reprinted).

——. *Andrew Boorde's Introduction and Dyetary.* London: N. Trubner & Co., 1870.

Gerard, John. *The Herball or General Historie of Plantes (1636).* London: The Minerva Press Ltd., 1971.

Harrison, William. *Harrison's Description of England in Shakespeare's Youth (1587).* London: New Shakespeare Society.

Hill, Thomas. *The Gardeners Labrynth (1594).* London: Garland Publishing Inc.

Holinshed's Chronicles of England. Volume IV. New York: AMS Press Inc, 1965 (reprinted).

Moryson, Fynes. *An Itenerary.* Volume IV (1617). Glasgow: James MacLehose and Sons.

Nichols, John Gough, ed. *The Diary of Henry Machin (1555–63).* London: J.B. Nichols and Son, 1870.

Parkinson, John. *Paradisi in Sole.* London, 1629.

Rye, William Brenchley, ed. *England as Seen by Foreigners.* London: John Russel Smith, 1865.

Stow, John. *A Survey of London, 1603.* Charles Lethbridge Kingsford, ed. Oxford: Oxford University Press, 1971 (reprinted).

Tusser, Thomas. *Five Hundred Pointes of Good Husbandry.* London, 1580.

Twyne, Thomas. *The Schoolemaster, or Teacher of Table Philosophy.* London, 1576.

Cookbooks

Dawson, Thomas. *The Good Huswifes Jewell.* London, 1596/97.

De Rosselli, Giovanne (trans.). *Epulario, or the Italian Banquet.* London, 1598.

Markham, Gervase. *The English Housewife.* London, 1615/1623.

May, Robert. *The Accomplisht Cook or The Art and Mystery of Cookery.* London, 1660.

Murrell, John. *A New Booke of Cookerie.* London, 1615.

———. *A Daily Exercise for Ladies and Gentlewomen.* London, 1617.

Partridge, John. *The Treasurie of Hidden Secrets.* London, 1633.

——— (attributed). *The Good Huswifes Handmaide for the Kitchin.* London, 1594.

Platt, Hugh. *The Jewell House of Art and Nature.* London, 1596.

———. *Sundrie New and Artificial Remedies Against Famine.* London, 1596.

———. *Delightes for Ladies.* London, 1617.

A Proper Newe Book of Cookrye. London, 1575.

W., A. *A Book of Cookrye.* London, 1591.

Woolley, Hannah. *The Accomplisht Ladys Delight.* London, 1672.

Index